CARAVAN
OF PAIN

The True Story of the
Tattoo the Earth Tour

SCOTT ALDERMAN

I have tried to recreate events, locales, and conversations from my memories of them. In order to maintain their anonymity, in some instances I have changed the names of individuals and places, and I may have changed some identifying characteristics and details such as physical properties, occupations, and places of residence.

Design by Edgar

Jacket photo by Fran Strine

ISBN: 978-0-578-34424-9

10 9 8 7 6 5 4 3 2 1

For Sparrow

Contents

Acknowledgments

Lisa Kaufman for being a much better editor than I deserve; Betsy Sparrow for reading and advice; Steve Edgar for design and Photoshop wizardry; Bruce Henkelmann for reading and kibitzing; Barry Lyons for proofreading; Shannon Larkin, Ruyter Suys, Blaine Cartwright, Naomi Fabricant, Fran Strine, Mike Bellamy, John French, Sean E. Demott, Ron Hausfeld, Dale Resteghini, and Josh Villella for interviews; the Stones and the Who for changing my life; and most importantly, to my son John Jasper, because I never want to miss an opportunity to needlessly pander to him.

Preface

November 2021

The couple of years leading up to Tattoo the Earth were the most tumultuous of my life. Never wrapped all that tight in the first place, I was collapsing under the stress, and it was evident that something was going to pop. I thought it might be an aneurysm, or my head rocketing completely off my shoulders, but what came out was the idea for Tattoo the Earth. Why an idea for a show combining tattoo and music, and not, say, a desire to feed the world, or a new type of dry cleaning bag? I have some theories, but I'm still not exactly sure why. I had just started collecting tattoos, but was not part of the culture. I'd been out of the music business for a long time, and had no desire to get back into it. Simply put, I cracked, and eighteen months later I was on stage at Giants Stadium.

I look at that time before Tattoo the Earth critically, especially about my work, and can't understand why I made some of the decisions I made, or trusted the people I trusted. Like most people, whenever I look back at myself, or write about the past, I always cringe a bit, maybe because of what I was wearing, or who I was with,

3

or especially if I did something that was embarrassing, or that didn't turn out how I'd hoped. I felt some of that as I wrote this book. But I felt no self-consciousness at all between the time I had the idea for Tattoo the Earth, and the day it became a reality, and I still find it hard to judge how I acted back then. There is a clear point of delineation. After the idea occurred to me, I entered a state of beatitude, at least I thought that's what it felt like at the time, in which everything I did was in service and devotion to the idea. And even though I know that poor shmuck is headed for a world of hurt, I can't bring myself to judge him. He was right about a lot of it—including tattoo becoming a mainstream cultural force.

Tattoo was still underground twenty years ago, still illegal in some states, and there were not a whole lot of mainstream personalities with tattoos. Look at a picture of the 2000 Olympic basketball team—not a tattoo to be found. If someone was heavily tattooed back then, they were most likely a hipster, a biker, a metal or hip hop musician, or a wrestler. Now the manager of my bank is covered in tattoos, as are Olympic gold medalists, and most sports and music stars; it is mind blowing to see how ubiquitous tattooing has become.

I was also right about Slipknot. They have remained one of the biggest metal bands in the world. In fact the whole metal genre is so durable that I could put on the same show with the same line-up today, and it would be huge. Metal fans' devotion to the lifestyle is as deep as that of tattoo aficionados for the tattoo lifestyle, and combining them created something special. I knew Slipknot's fans were in it for the long term.

My goal in writing this book was to tell a story about a vision quest, and a crazy music business story that marks an interesting time in our culture and history. But as I wrote it I realized it is also the story of being broken. It's the story of how Tattoo the Earth saved me when I really needed saving.

"It was sad to see his tall figure as we drove away, just like the other figures in New York and New Orleans; they stand uncertainly underneath immense skies, and everything about them is drowned."

– Jack Kerouac, *On the Road*

Chapter One

Triple X Tattoo

I had the idea for what was to become Tattoo the Earth at 3:45pm on November 18, 1998, at Triple X Tattoo in New York City. Sean Vasquez was finishing a tattoo on my calf that he'd started a few weeks earlier in New Orleans, and we were continuing a conversation about what I should do next with my life. My business career had just gone bust in spectacular fashion, and I wanted to do something unusual, something that had never been done before, something like the greatest freak show ever, like a giant S&M Woodstock, or a festival that combined tattooing and body art with rock bands.

"I'll call it Tattoo the Earth," I blurted out.

Sean stopped tattooing my leg and looked up at me, his glasses slipping down on his nose. The sudden silence of his machine stopping and the absence of pain made it feel like I'd stepped into another dimension. I took a deep breath. I've had a few epiphanies like this in my life. The last had been ten years prior, when I knew it was time to get off drugs. For a long while, anyways. I'd said, "I'm done," and quit cold turkey. This time I said, "Tattoo the Earth."

I kept riffing on the idea while Sean finished the tattoo, envisioning what Tattoo the Earth would look like and feel like, what bands might play it, which tattoo artists would be there, could it be done outside, can you tattoo outside, and on and on. After he finished my tattoo, Sean and I went to Dental Domination Night at an underground nightclub in the meatpacking district called Mother. Mother was a trip. They threw parties like Click + Drag, Meat, and the Clit Club, and would soon close as gentrification crept from SoHo and Tribeca into their neighborhood. It was just like what had happened in the East Village the previous decade, when developers wiped out a whole host of clubs and bars along with the lovable, degenerate character of these places.

While two dominatrixes dressed as nurses fake-pulled a tooth from a writhing patient with a giant pair of pliers, I was spewing out Tattoo the Earth ideas as if possessed. Shouting in Sean's ear to overcome blaring techno and dental screams, I laid out a whole plan for a type of tattoo festival that had never been done before. Sean did tattoo conventions all over the world, so he knew what was already out there. What I was talking about, a mainstream tattoo and music festival, had never been attempted before. Nothing even close.

I'd met Sean six months earlier, the morning I told my boss (and best friend) to go fuck himself, quit my job, and walked across West 36th Street to Sean's shop, Triple X Tattoo. There Sean inscribed a tribal tattoo on my left wrist—the first tattoo I'd gotten that wasn't hidden by my T-shirt—to commemorate that pivotal moment in my life, one I hoped would lead to positive changes. He'd opened his shop right after the law banning tattooing in New York City had been overturned the year before. The ban had been enacted in 1961 after a Hepatitis B outbreak, though there was scant evidence tattooing had anything to do with the outbreak. Tattooing was considered a gutter business and an easy target for a public health victory. For the next 36 years, tattooing in the five boroughs took place in illegal shops and private apartments, unregulated and underground.

I'd walked past Sean's shop hundreds of times going in and out of my office, but on that day I was inside and Sean was there at the front desk. Though he didn't usually take customers without an appointment, he had some time, and before I knew it he was working on my wrist. Triple X Tattoo had a fantastic vibe, and I dug it the minute I walked the one flight up a narrow staircase and entered. The waiting area was bohemian and super chill; Sean's partner was a fine artist, and his artwork—including many enormous pieces inspired by traditional tattoo art—hung all over the walls. There were also various examples of carny tattoo memorabilia, and a giant green velvet sofa that swallowed you whole. Even though Sean's own shop rules specified that pot was to be smoked on the fire escape right outside his workspace in the back, he usually smoked inside and the whole shop constantly reeked of cannabis and hash; it reminded me of the coffee shops in Amsterdam. The shop was designed for people to hang out and get comfortable, and that's exactly what everyone did.

Sean tattooed in the back office, and he held court there like a Buddha. He'd close his door, but people were constantly stopping in to talk or get high or just hang, so eventually he'd just leave it open. Everyone wanted to be with Sean, and his office was always filled with clients, friends, dealers, other artists, apprentices, or anyone who fell into his orbit. Sean had that thing that just attracted people to him—women, men, platonic crushes, fans—and he knew how to handle it. I'd had success as a promoter and club owner in the music business when I was younger, and Sean reminded me of a rock star; one of those people who knew everyone wanted to suck his dick but also knew how to handle it without becoming a total jerk. He was my age, around forty, Hispanic, tall, with vivid green eyes. He was a commanding presence: graying temples and goatee, large plugs in his ears, tattoos all over his body, including a tribal piece hand-tattooed with a stick on his Adam's apple. He looked like a badass, and he was, but he was also intelligent and cerebral, soft-spoken and vulnerable, and oozed sexuality. Sean had left his wife, kid, and regular boring job to become a tattoo artist, travel the world, and finally be the person he had always wanted to be. He had exceeded his expectations and was now one of the leading artists in the world. Sean was just what I needed at that point in my life. His empathy, and his focus while he was tattooing, made him a skilled listener. Tattoo artists were like piano players and place kickers: You hold on tight when you find a good one. I was content to just get tattoos from Sean for the rest of my life, and the bonus was I also found a friend, though I wasn't sure I wanted a new one.

I had just had my greatest professional success, but was betrayed by my closest friend. I met Jeff in drug rehab in 1987, and we clicked immediately. We were the same age, grew up in the same town, liked the same music, and were both strung out on drugs. We stayed clean in Narcotics Anonymous, and became inseparable over the next ten years. We were the best man at each other's weddings. We were like brothers. After a time I started working at the consulting company he owned, which was growing at a rapid pace. I found success there, and the combined goal of building something big and great only seemed to bring us closer together. Jeff became wealthy when the company went public. I did okay, and was poised to run the entire thing, when I found out he'd lied to me and had screwed me out of a significant amount of money. I had never been anything but loyal to him, and devoted to his family and business, and I was fucking devastated. And though my wife Betsy had been saying for months beforehand that he was going to screw me, and I saw him doing it to everyone else, I never thought he would do it to me. And for no reason other than greed and to exert control. He thought I'd shake it off because of our friendship, and be grateful for what I got, but I told him to fuck off, and never spoke to him again.

***

Back at Mother, Sean Vasquez and I were drunk talk-shouting over music and screams, spraying warm Jägermeister into each other's ears from the shots we were pounding late into the night.

"I could do this," I told him, grabbing him by the shoulders.

"You could totally do this."

"You really think so?"

"I know it, bro," he said back, grabbing my shoulders and bringing me closer to him, closing his eyes in his way and pulling my forehead to touch his, "You can do this."

"This is why we met, so you could do this with me."

"I know, bro. I know."

***

I got my first tattoo in 1991 when I was thirty years old and four years clean and sober. Tattoos weren't a thing for me growing up because my idols didn't have them. As a teenager, I was so enamored of my rock heroes that if Keith Richards or Pete Townsend had tattoos, I would have absolutely gotten one. Instead I associated tattoos with bikers and convicts. I also didn't like the sight of my own blood, needles, or pain, so tattoos were never on my radar. I was all about rebellion and living like an outsider, but tattoos had such a negative connotation for me that I saw nothing but pain and losers.

Until I went to graduate school at UC Berkeley, and met a group of sober freaks in San Francisco who were heavily into tattooing and piercing, and who would regularly make fun of me for my East Coast vanity and squeamishness. People on the West Coast were much freer with their bodies and sexuality, and the longer I lived out there the more I started to get more comfortable with mine. As a goof, they bought me a copy of *Re/Search #12: Modern Primitives*, a seminal book that chronicled the history of body modification from ancient times to the present. Some of the piercings were hard to stomach, and my friends took glee in seeing my reactions as I leafed through it (I didn't even like having a zipper on my jeans). Every type of tattoo, scarification, implant, and body manipulation imaginable was depicted, and much of it was fascinating. I read the chapter on an old tattoo artist named Lyle Tuttle, and I was fascinated by the picture of him being tattooed by hand with a stick in Samoa; lying on his stomach, blissfully staring at the camera like someone was rubbing suntan oil on his back at the beach. In another section, on traditional tribal tattoos from Samoa, Borneo, and New Zealand, one of the tribal tattoos from the Philippines caught my eye, and I bookmarked the page.

A short time later my father died, and a few months after that I decided to get that tribal design from the Philippines tattooed on my arm. It was small and shaped like an arc, with cog-like juts coming out of it; I wanted it on my upper arm curving to the shape of my shoulder. I wasn't exactly sure what my motivation was. It might have been to commemorate the loss, or maybe to reclaim my body after watching my father's get ravaged by cancer, or to prove to myself that I could take the pain if I had to. Technically, it meant that I couldn't be buried in a Jewish cemetery, and though that was certainly a selling point, the simple explanation was that I saw the design in a book and wanted it on me. My sponsor in Narcotics Anonymous had beautiful color tattoos on his arms, like brushed watercolor, and over the years he'd educated me about the history and possibilities of tattooing. He'd been telling me for years that I was going to eventually get one, and was bursting when I told him I'd decided to. He recommended his favorite artist, Shotsie Gorman. I had to make the appointment weeks in advance, which gave me a lot of time to think and worry about it. When the day arrived I was a bag of nerves. I was fine with other people's pain and blood—I'd seen every manner of bodily fluid and horror when I worked at an AIDS hospice in Greenwich Village during the heart of the pandemic—but the sight of my own blood made me sweaty and woozy. Blood tests, gashed knees, and deep cuts could render me wobbly.

Shotsie's tattoo shop was in a strip mall off Route 9 in Wayne, New Jersey. It was my first time inside a tattoo shop, and it was much more mundane than I'd imagined, like a funky hair salon with bad lighting. Tattoo designs called "flash" hung all over the walls in large sheets. There was every style imaginable: Traditional with bold, colorful images of roses, anchors, and hearts with "Mother" in them; tribal from every corner of the globe; Japanese, with large historical stories featuring dragons and ancient lore; New School, with its fusing of many styles and art school sensibility; and any other style you could conceive of. There was a small waiting area, and four or five rooms for tattooing; the place smelled like a cross between incense and antiseptic soap. Shotsie was a bit gruff, like I was inconveniencing him. I got the feeling he was doing my tattoo as a favor to my sponsor, and would typically give a job as simple as my tattoo to a junior artist. But he seemed competent and professional, and ready to get it done. I brought in a copy of the design I wanted, and he used tattoo transfer paper to make a stencil of it, and then placed an impression of it on my arm to use as a guide (and to make sure the placement and size was right). The stencil ink rubs right off the skin if it's not right, and he did a few before we agreed on the placement.

First, he was going to use a tattoo machine with a single needle to do the outline, and then a machine with multiple needles to fill in the black. The tattoo machine has barely changed from the original notion of a rotary stencil pen invented by Thomas Edison in 1876. In 1891, Samuel Reilly invented a machine based on Edison's that delivered ink into the skin instead of onto a piece of paper. In 1929, Percy Waters invented the electromagnetic tattoo machine with coils that vibrate, and that machine, with some minor improvements over the years, is the most commonly used today. The magnet makes the coil vibrate, and that pushes the needles up and down like pistons. Shotsie's set up was neat and clean, and you could tell he had done this a thousand times. He wore gloves, everything was individually wrapped, and there was a big autoclave that sterilized the equipment between uses. Though the medical compliance reassured me that I was in a safe environment, it also made me a bit nauseous.

My first thought when the tattoo machine hit my skin was: Hey, that doesn't hurt that much. It felt like someone was scratching my arm, and I was relieved the pain wasn't a big deal, and tried to relax. But it was too late to quell my anxiety, and within minutes I almost fainted and was lying on the floor doing yoga breathing while Shotsie daubed my head with a cold compress. I was eventually able to pull myself together and get the piece finished, but it was embarrassing. Shotsie was a top artist, and usually did big complex color tattoos, and I went down because of a four inch by half-inch simple tribal tattoo on my upper bicep. The time I was on the floor recuperating was longer than the tattoo took to finish, but Shotsie was cool and didn't make a big deal about it (and I gave him a huge tip).

I loved the tattoo. The way it looked, the way it curved along the top of my arm, the contrast of the black ink against my skin, and just the way it felt knowing that it was there. It was covered by my T-shirt sleeve, so I'd need to show it to someone for them to see it, but I hadn't gotten it for anyone else. I'd gotten it for me, and despite having told people I only wanted the one tattoo, six months later I got another one at a shop in Virginia—a Japanese kanji symbol for peace below my tribal piece. And a few months after that I got the kanji symbol for fighting below the other one. All three tattoos were above my T-shirt sleeve line, and only poked below it if I moved a certain way; I didn't want to go below that and wasn't sure about my other arm. The next tattoo was a piece on the side of my calf that was supposed to look like Mercury's wing, but looked more like I'd rubbed my leg up against some wet black paint that had left a smudge. I didn't do any research on these tattoo shops or artists. I'd just walk in, pick out a design, and get it from the next available artist, and typically they were the younger ones who didn't quite know what they were doing. Tattooing is a craft, and the depth the ink is injected into the skin is crucial for look and longevity of the tattoo. One of the Kanji tribal tattoos is still raised and bumpy 30 years later.

Sean chuckled when I first showed him my budding collection because it seems everyone's first tattoos suck. Sean did his first tattoo to himself with a sewing needle, and he showed me the barely distinguishable squiggly lines underneath his now fully tattooed arm. After Sean did a few tribal pieces on my right arm, including a black tribal piece on my right bicep with the red Rolling Stones tongue logo entwined in it, I asked him to fix the tattoo on my calf with a cover-up. A good artist can incorporate a bad design into a bigger new design, and most times you can't even recognize the original tattoo. Sean said he was going to be attending the New Orleans Tattoo Convention on Halloween weekend, and asked if my wife Betsy and I wanted to join him. We'd hang in New Orleans, he'd do my cover-up, and I'd get to see what a tattoo convention was all about.

Betsy and I had never been to New Orleans, and we desperately needed a break. We had been together four years, had recently married, and then my mother got cancer and died young, and then her mother got a terrible cancer diagnosis, and then one of my oldest friends got sick. I had relapsed after ten years clean, wasn't sure if I wanted to be clean anymore, and was surprisingly comfortable with that decision. I started smoking pot regularly again, much to Betsy's chagrin. She was not only concerned about where smoking pot might lead, but she didn't smoke, and thought it might create a wedge between us. I was also playing in high stakes poker games, and was working insane hours taking the consulting company public. After I quit my job, we bought a house in the country in Central Massachusetts to be near her mother. The real estate agent who sold us the house was obligated to disclose that a previous owner had alleged an alien abduction at the house, but assured us that the person also alleged abductions in other locations, so the house was safe. We weren't sure about the house, but that sealed the deal for us. Our property included a one acre plowed field that looked like a landing pad, and we'd have fires at night waiting for visitors. Leaving New York City was good for us. We remodeled the house and looked to the future. Betsy liked Sean and the people hanging around his shop; they were more authentic than the people I'd been hanging out with before I quit my job and had varied interests and beliefs. My work in the corporate world had involved many social obligations that Betsy had hated; she was always bored by the one-dimensional banal conversations she had to endure.

In New Orleans, Betsy and I spent Halloween day visiting one of the Saint Louis aboveground cemeteries—visiting cemeteries was one of our things—and a voodoo shop nearby. That night we hung out with Sean and his friends. Bourbon Street was a madhouse, and though I was kind of over drunken crowds by that point in my life, Betsy and I got loaded and had a great time. The next day we went to the convention so Sean could do the cover up. I hadn't been to a tattoo convention before, but once you got over the initial novelty of it, it was unremarkable except for the fact that inside the dozens of pipe-and-drape booths lining the hotel ballroom floor, people were getting tattooed. Streams of people who weren't getting tattooed moved through the tight aisles checking out the artists. There were some vendors selling jewelry and clothing, but once you got through the maze of booths there wasn't much else to see. If it wasn't for the music, and the buzzing and bleeding, you would think you were at a plumbing fixtures convention.

My tattoo should have taken an hour or so, but halfway through I started feeling lightheaded and queasy. A sheen of sweat appeared above my upper lip, and then my mind started racing. Betsy recognized these telltale signs, and looked over at me nervously. It was stuffy in the convention center, and loud; the buzzing of dozens of tattoo machines was now drowned out by a live rock band playing twenty feet away from Sean's booth. The experience was like getting a medical procedure in the first row at a rock concert. The walls of the booth were only three or four feet high, and people kept streaming by to check Sean's portfolio, and see what he was putting on me. I felt like I was in a zoo, and it started freaking me out. I felt like the whole convention hall was starting to spin around me. A guy came by to say hello to Sean who was tattooed from head to toe. He was wearing shorts and no shirt, and there wasn't an inch of him that wasn't tattooed, including his face. There was so much it was hard to discern one image or piece from another. He had pus globules tattooed in his armpits that dripped down his arm. He was the freakiest person I'd ever seen, and he and Sean knew each other from going to tattoo conventions. At one point, the guy took his dick out to show Sean a checkerboard he had tattooed on it, and that's when I started feeling untethered.

I tried to continue, but Sean could see I was struggling and suggested a break. I told him that the noise and heat and commotion were freaking me out, as well as the checkerboard dick, and that I didn't want to continue. He understood, and said we could finish it at his shop when we got back to New York. Betsy was turned off by the whole thing, and thought Mr. Checkerboard Dick was a loser (though still more interesting than the jerks from my corporate work). I cautioned her not to disparage him when we met with Sean and some other tattoo artists later that night. It was our first convention, and we were new to tattoo culture, and I didn't want to come off as disrespectful or judgmental. We were both relieved when Sean told us he thought the guy was completely nuts and fucked up, not at all representative of the tattoo community. I wasn't so sure, but it didn't matter. I wasn't in the tattoo business, and didn't see myself going to any more conventions.

That is, until Sean was finishing the tattoo he started and I had the idea for Tattoo the Earth. When I got home from Mother that first night after having the idea, I wrote out my vision in a manic frenzy, like I was taking dictation. I came up with a detailed plan, and a framework for starting multiple businesses connected to tattooing. Fresh off being part of the team that took the consulting company public, I knew what had to be done to create a story, and what kind of financial plan people would invest in. I listened to music and wrote furiously on a legal pad in between bouts of crying, heaving, guttural body-shaking sobs like I'd never experienced before. And not of sadness, but of relief and gratitude. I felt centered and integrated for the first time in my life. I had clarity and purpose. Within a few days, I had a twenty-page pitch book detailing my plan, and a clear vision of what I wanted to create. The pitch book contained an overview of the festival, tattoo industry demographics, magazine ads and celebrity photos featuring tattoos. It was difficult finding ads featuring body art, and there were still not many celebrities sporting tattoos in 1998 (my list included Alan Iverson, Kaiser Wilhelm, and Oetzi the 5,300-year-old frozen iceman). Tattooing was barely above ground, and barely in the mainstream. But I was going to change all that.

Chapter Two

Cocksuckers and Copycats

One hallmark of my campaign to get Tattoo the Earth off the ground, right from the onset, was that anyone I pitched the idea to, or anyone who saw the pitch book, gave me the best contacts they had. Many times they would call the person themselves and put them right on the phone to talk to me. People immediately believed in the idea, and in my ability to pull it off, and wanted to do everything they could do to help make it real. Sean was the first one. He loved the pitch book when I next saw him and told me he'd been thinking about nothing else since our night of drunken inspiration. He also said that our first stop had to be with Lyle Tuttle, one of the tattoo artists I'd learned about in *Modern Primitives*, the book my Berkeley friends had given me. Lyle had been one of Sean's mentors, and Sean was confident he would want to be involved. There was a tattoo convention the following week in Richmond, Virginia, that Lyle would be attending, so we booked some flights and planned our meeting with him.

Lyle Tuttle was fourteen in 1946 when he saw the troops return from WWII, and seeing their tattoos inspired him to get one himself—a heart with "Mother" tattooed on his arm. Lyle once said, "Show me a man with a tattoo and I'll show you an interesting past," and his past was the stuff of legend. A few years after getting that first tattoo, he was tattooing professionally, and traveled the world to learn all he could about all the different styles of tattooing. Lyle opened his first shop in San Francisco in 1960 and made it his life's work to get tattooing out of the back alleys and into mainstream acceptance.

Though Lyle may have been inspired by the WWII vets coming home, their wives and girlfriends were less appreciative, and tattooing would have disappeared entirely after the war if not for biker gangs in California, New York, and Europe. The artistry and technology kept evolving to greater levels in the 1960s and 1970s, but tattooing as a business and industry had not progressed much since the biker gangs of 1950s. Lyle helped change that. He tattooed the likes of Janis Joplin, Joan Baez, Henry Fonda, and Cher (he did the famous tattoo on her ass cheek) and was featured on a cover of *Rolling Stone*. There was still a shop in Lyle's name in San Francisco, but by the time I met him he was done tattooing—except occasionally when he'd get a large fee to tattoo his signature on someone—and devoted his energy toward building his brand. He spent most of his time traveling to tattoo conventions, doing clinics, selling his custom tattoo machines and flash, and enjoying his status as the "grandfather of modern tattooing."

The Richmond convention was held in the nondescript ballroom of a cheap hotel that was even grimmer than the convention hall in New Orleans. We walked the convention floor, and just like in New Orleans, Sean knew everyone, and everyone respected him. Other tattoo artists and fans were surprised to see him there and not tattooing and were intrigued when he told them we were there to meet Lyle. I watched one of the tattoo contests, with categories like best black and grey, best sleeve color, best back piece, best portrait, etc. The tattoos were judged on their artwork and craft, not on the attractiveness of the body they were on, and that was a nice part of tattoo conventions: Anyone with a great tattoo could win a contest.

A short time later, the legend was sitting in front of me. He was almost seventy, his girlfriend was thirty-ish, and he was nursing a vodka and grapefruit juice. He wore tan pants and had his shirt off. The upper part of his body suit was incredible, though his arms were so tattooed it was difficult to distinguish what was what. His chest was a mix of tribal and modern tattooing that stopped at his neck along the line of a T-shirt. He had nothing on his neck or hands; he could wear a suit and tie and look like a retired insurance salesman. With his shirt off in a shitty hotel room in Richmond, he looked like a fucking pirate.

Lyle listened patiently while I told him about the idea, barely looking at the pitch book as he flipped through it. Other than an occasional snort, he looked at me with the excitement of a bored grandpa who was missing discount frozen yogurt night at the mall on account of me. I told him about my background, my work in music, my recent corporate work, and how much tattoos meant to me. I also told him about my first tattoo and my seeing his picture in *Modern Primitives*. I was naked compared to Lyle and Sean, and I got the sense Lyle thought I was a poser, someone who got a few tattoos and saw a way to make money. I could tell he was irritated right from the get-go.

"I see this festival like a Woodstock for the body art generation," I told him. "The connection between the tattoo artists, bands, and fans is powerful; forged in blood, ink, and music. That's one part. I also want to tie in museums, and academia, and mainstream sponsors to put tattooing in the forefront."

Sean told him some of the artists we would want to have involved and how we would treat the artists like a band—and on the same level as the music. We would take tattooing out of hotel ballrooms, and put it right in the middle of a massive cultural event.

"This is a natural continuation of the work you've been doing your entire life," I told him, "And we want you to be part of it."

I'd been talking too long, verbally dancing for my life, and finally paused to light a joint and gauge his reaction. He stared at the pitch book for a while.

"You are completely full of shit!" he bellowed. "You think you'll get tattooists to work together, to put aside their egos for something created by an outsider?"

"Well, I am full of shit," I shot back. "I think you need to be full of shit to pull something like this off. And yes, I think we can unite the tattoo artists to work together with us."

"Tattoo artists are all cocksuckers and copycats," he barked at me. "And that will never change."

I could tell we were done, and Sean and I wrapped it up. We were prepared to give Lyle a piece of the tour if he joined us, but instead I gave him an ounce of some amazing pot as a tribute and thanked him for his time.

Sean had told me that tattoo artists were a paranoid and wary group, but I hadn't been fully prepared for a snootful of it on my first meeting. I know Sean was disappointed by the meeting, too; he said he thought Lyle would come around once it all came together, and we had bands attached. But Lyle was right: I had approached him too soon, before I knew what I was talking about. His skepticism did not deter me, but made clear that I needed to hone my narrative and prioritize the music part of the project. Sean was dejected when we got back to New York, so I gave him $5,000 as a show of confidence that he was my key guy. Sean and I were in total sync, and I didn't want him wavering.

I dropped almost $30,000 in the first weeks after having the idea. I put a lawyer on a retainer to put together contracts—including one for Sean—and hired another law firm to do trademarking. I bought a mid-length black leather Calvin Klein jacket (like the one DeNiro wore in *Mean Streets*), a new laptop and cell phone, a pound of some mind-blowing pot—all the things I would need to travel the world in pursuit of my goal. I decided to stay at the Plaza when I was in New York, which was expensive at first, but became more reasonable over the months as I got to know the management. My thought was that I had a million dollar idea, and needed to look like someone who could pull it off. I never once said I was going to put the money up for the tour. That would cost millions, and I didn't have that. But I knew that if I got the right band, promoter, celebrity, or whatever, that the money would follow. I had enough money to get the money I would need. My focus was on getting a band attached, or some other entity, that would make a deal attractive to investors. JP Morgan told people he wouldn't lend them money, but he would walk down the street with them, and that's what I was searching for.

Though my focus switched to the music side, Sean and I did go to Berlin a few weeks later for another tattoo convention. Sean said European conventions were much better than the ones in the U.S., and that I should experience a good one. Plus, Bernie Luther would be there, and Bernie was one of the artists Sean wanted to recruit for Tattoo the Earth. He also wanted Bernie to start a tribal sleeve for me. Bernie was from Austria and was part of a new wave of artists from Europe, including Filip Leu and Tin Tin, that had taken tattoo to another level. Bernie's freehand artistry, use of color, and fusing multiple styles into a single tattoo—like Japanese, tribal, and traditional tattoos juxtaposed on the skin so the styles don't clash but become something unique—had placed him at the top of the tattoo world. Going to hundreds of conventions on five continents had earned him the nickname, "Traveling Bernie," and Sean said a tattoo tour wouldn't be worth shit without Bernie on it.

Sean was right about the Berlin Convention. It was far and away better than the ones I'd seen in the U.S. It was in an expo hall with many levels, and the quality and diversity of the vendors—some tattooists hailed from Japan and Borneo—was at a whole other level.

There were bands playing but in other parts of the complex, so the sound wasn't overwhelming. Hash smoke hung in the air, and the whole vibe was welcoming and conducive to lingering and exploring.

Sean got some hand tattooing done on his knuckles. The tattooist used a small hammer and a stick with needles attached to it, and he would gently tap the stick into the skin to deposit the ink. The guy who did Sean's knuckles wanted to do mine, but I declined. I wanted to be able to wear a long sleeve shirt or suit and not be a tattooed person. Plus, I was certain I would stand in front of a judge again in my life, and I didn't want neck or hand tattoos influencing someone's impression of me. But the idea of hand tattooing intrigued me, and a few weeks later I got the Japanese symbol for "sparrow"—Betsy's last name—hand poked into my arm by a tattooist using a stick with needles attached. It was actually less painful than getting tattooed by machine and quieter, and I wanted more of it.

We met Bernie on the convention floor. He shared Lyle Tuttle's distrust of outsiders, but he was warmer and more expansive. Bernie was a skater kid who grew up on the streets of Vienna and London. He had long un-washed brown hair, and looked like a hippie. Bernie's shop was located in Vienna, but he traveled constantly, to the farthest reaches of the planet. He could fashion a bong out of anything: an old can, just about any piece of fruit, or the earth itself. He'd once stopped on the side of a deserted highway, and using some water made a bong in the dirt, like a sandcastle, and lied down next to it with a rolled-up bill to get a hit of some hash. He told us he'd had a fire at his house in Mali, got his girlfriend and kid out safely, then ran back in to see what he could save. The house was engulfed, and he had no time. He thought about grabbing the $10,000 he had in cash, or his tattoo designs, but decided to save his favorite pair of boots instead. They were cool boots, brown and beaten, the laces barely holding them together.

I trusted Sean's judgment, and I gave Bernie my left arm without conditions. We got high all night while Bernie drew a tribal design on my arm with a Bic pen. The design incorporated a mix of tribal styles, with geometric swirls and shapes that used open skin space to accentuate the design. In keeping with the black and white theme of the tribal pieces Sean did on me, Bernie used black, grey, and white ink, and then outlined the entire piece, filling in enough, so it looked finished enough until I could see him the next time. He tattooed me right up until I had to leave for the airport. I hadn't slept for two days by then, and I was bleeding, sore, and catatonic on the flight home. Bernie had started an epic tattoo, and we had connected, but I could see that Lyle Tuttle was right. It was going to be hard to deal with tattoo artists. They were not interested in being handled or cajoled and would push back on anyone who tried.

After our tattoo adventures in Richmond and Berlin, I switched gears and concentrated on the music for the tour. Through some business contacts, I was introduced to two lawyers. It's always helpful to start with lawyers. They know everyone, and they get off on making connections. The first one, a mildly successful entertainment attorney who was then producing a documentary on the Yiddish language called *Our Maloshen*, liked the idea and introduced me to his best contact, Don Kirshner. The two of us met for drinks at the Oak Bar in the Plaza, and it was a mind fuck sitting across from him. In the 1950s and 1960s, Don Kirshner had been a key figure at the Brill Building songwriting hub; he was the mastermind behind the Monkees and their TV show. In the 1970s, there were only a few places on TV to see live rock music, and *Don Kirshner's Rock Concert* was one of them. I let him know how much the show meant to me as a teenager.

"Scott," he told me with his distinctive New York accent, "Tattoo the Earth isn't just an idea for a concert. You're talking about a whole industry here."

He smiled as he looked through the pitch book.

"I absolutely love this," he said, and offered to help in any way he could, though the meeting ultimately went nowhere.

"Look at the big picture, Scott" he told me several times. "It's a whole industry."

I'd already envisioned spin-off tattoo and retail shops, but after I met with him, I took it further, adding additional ideas to the pitch book to show the breadth and depth of the idea. I came up with an idea for a cartoon series called *T.H.A.T. Squad (Tattooed Heroes Against Tyranny)* about a group of inked superheroes whose tattoos come to life and help them fight evil in the universe. One character was a Jewish accountant whose portrait of his mother came to life, and annoyed enemies into submission. I came up with a magazine called *Ink Gun*, a website called Tat.Chat, and a plexi-glass tattoo booth with giant Lego-like modules called Festipod that I designed to travel on the road (I made a miniature prototype in my basement, using a Barbie doll to model as the tattoo artist).

The second music business lawyer, Stuart Silfen, was famous for his involvement in Woodstock, and for his industry connections. I had been having people sign non-disclosure agreements before I told them about the idea, and he laughed out loud when I said that.

"No one is going to steal this," he told me. "It will be hard to pull this off. No one else is thinking about this right now, and even if they were, it doesn't matter. Talk to anyone who'll listen. Anytime. Anywhere."

He chuckled as he leafed through the pitch book and kept saying how clever he thought it was. "Irving would love this," he said a few times, and offered to make a call on my behalf.

Irving was Irving Azoff, who was at the time, and still is, one of the most powerful people in music. He managed the Eagles, and at various times in his career was an agent, owned a record company and a music merchandising company, produced movies, ran Ticketmaster, and also ran Live Nation, the biggest concert promoter in the world. A few days later, I was on the phone with

Azoff. He got the concept, and wanted to hear more. A few weeks later, I was in Los Angeles to meet with him.

I was feeling fantastic. The driver who picked me up at the airport listened to my pitch (anyone, anytime, anywhere, right?) and told me how rich I was going to be; he said he saw lightning bolts in my eyes. As we drove, I saw a billboard for the new Rolling Stones live album, *No Security*, and it featured a woman covered in Sean's tattoos. A cosmic message from Sean, I thought, and I asked the car to stop at Tower Records so I could buy the CD.

I stayed in a bungalow at the Beverly Hills Hotel, put the Stones CD in the player in the room, got stoned, made some calls, and got psyched up for the meeting with Azoff. By the time the last song, "Out of Control," came on, volume on high, I was overcome with emotions, just as I had been the night I'd first thought of Tattoo the Earth. I was sobbing, singing, dancing, and genuflecting. Anyone who saw me and didn't know I was an atheist might have thought I was experiencing a religious conversion. I was overwhelmed with waves of gratitude, and I played the song over and over again, cranking it louder each time. A similar thing had happened a few weeks earlier where I had to pull the car off the road while listening to a Who song. Music seemed to be the trigger, and though music always had a powerful affect me, I'd never felt like this, even during my fun hard drug-using days. I was a blubbering mess, but I was completely sure of my place on the planet. My feet were planted. I was grateful. All the different parts of me were coalescing: the freak, the suit, the junkie, the carny, the writer. All of it.

It did occur to me that I could be having a psychotic break of some kind. I'd read an article about the top life stressors a person can experience, and I'd experienced almost all of them in the previous two years. I'd suffered from depression my whole life (I see now it was the underlying foundation of my addiction), but it wasn't until I was in my early thirties that I found a shrink who broke it down for me. He said I had multiple levels of depression. I had a low-grade depression since childhood that was like a mild hum constantly on in the background. I had an existential depression, an Eastern European darkness that formed my sensibility (this depression, I liked). And lastly, I had a cyclical depression that affected me a few times a year and could lay me low for weeks on end. The last type was the type that could fuck up my life, even if I took medication. I had always been moody and had a manic kind of energy (I was a speed freak when I was teenager), but this type of manic state was something new. It did occur to me I could just finally be cracking up. But then I thought: Fuck it. I could be losing it, but I was inspired, and I was inspiring other people of note and substance, and no one was treating me like I was nuts.

By the time I hit Azoff's office, though, I wasn't feeling it anymore. I was used to depression switching on and off, but I'd never gone from such a high to such a low so quickly. I could tell I wasn't connecting with him. I can remember every detail of the meeting—the surprising plainness of his waiting area, the memorabilia in his office, what he was wearing, and the way I was sunk into the chair—but barely a word of our conversation. He got someone on the phone to inquire about the Red Hot Chili Peppers, then told me they weren't a functioning band at the time (which turned out to be false). I sat there feeling like a phony. It occurred to me that I was fucking chum. I hadn't put enough blood and guts into the project, and I wasn't at a level in the music business where I could just throw an idea out there and have it stick. I was an outsider, just like with tattooing, and I sensed the same wariness and defensiveness. Azoff said to give him some time to think about it. Betsy and I returned to LA a few weeks later, but Azoff couldn't meet with me. He did put me in touch with a top concert promoter, Concerts West, but they'd had a bad experience with tattooing at previous events, and took a hard pass.

After some promising meetings, I was back at the beginning. But I had learned a ton, and realized I had to change the format. My original idea was for a three-day festival like Woodstock, but a marketing research company I hired told me that those types of multi-day festivals were going out of style. Despite the success of the Lollapalooza festival, three-day festivals were too risky because people were sleeping over, which is always dangerous (riots broke out at Woodstock 1999), and weather could ruin the whole thing. Tours were safer because you had multiple shows to overcome the bad ones. But it was going to be difficult to get a major band to commit to 30 or 40 shows with an unproven concept because if the concept failed, the band's brand would get dragged down with it. The owner of the marketing company told me that one in a hundred ideas like mine ever become reality, and he didn't think mine was the one.

"You just wait and see," I told him.

My main takeaway from the first few months hawking Tattoo the Earth was that everyone had flipped over the concept, and my pitch for the project was getting better. My utter belief in the idea gave it authenticity, and it was apparent to all I met that I was serious and driven. Within weeks of having the idea, Tattoo the Earth had gotten me in front of Lyle Tuttle and Irving Azoff, and that was not nothing. Plus, I now had a tattoo sleeve from Bernie Luther that made me feel invincible. There was someone or something out there that was going to make it happen, and now I knew I had the ability to get to the people who could help me find the thing that would light the rocket. That was positive. I could build off that. I retreated to Massachusetts to regroup.

Chapter Three

The Vomiting Demographic

The end of my first attempt to launch Tattoo the Earth coincided with my annual February depression, and I had some dark nights of the soul. Rationally and intellectually, I knew my idea was good, and I knew I had a chance to pull it off. But in the depths of that depression I felt like the whole thing was folly, and that I was embarrassing myself running around the world on a losing proposition. Just as I sensed that much of the euphoria I was feeling wasn't real, I knew from lugging my depression around my entire life that I just needed to ride the episode out and to try not make any major decisions or send an ill-advised email while it was happening. Doing a project with depression is like running a race with weights on your legs; it takes twice as much energy to get to the same place. I'd spent a lot of money, hadn't worked for almost a year, and I was starting to feel some financial pressure. At no point did I ever think of stopping. I just needed to retool, which was difficult when I felt so shitty. I made calls, and set up meetings and a strategy for my next push. I spoke to the music writer Bob Grossweiner, who suggested the tag line "The Rock & Ink Tour," which I adopted immediately, and that I contact Kevin Lyman, the founder of the Warped Tour, and Jack Utisck, an independent promoter in Miami. I also had a plan to raise some start-up money, and I booked a flight to Vienna for Betsy and me so I could have Bernie Luther finish my tattoo and she could have a change of scene.

After a few weeks I was ready to get back to NYC. My new plan involved pacing myself, cutting back on traveling, and saving money by staying at a middling hotel in Midtown instead of the Plaza. Betsy was heading to Florida to be with her family and stopped in NYC the night before I was due to arrive. She stayed at our new hotel, and as I was winding down the Taconic on my way to NYC, phoned to report on its cheap sheets and rancid KitKats in the vending machine. Homey isn't playing this game, I thought, and changed course directly back to the Plaza. Fuck it, I thought. I'm all in, and if it all goes south at least I'll be comfortable.

Another part of my new plan was to go directly to the bands, but I'd been to only a handful of concerts in the past ten years and was pretty out of touch. Music had been an integral part of my addiction, and I'd pulled away from it and the music business when I got clean. I'd started in the music business at eighteen when, after getting thrown out of college, I got a job at a rock club. Over the next few years, I became a road manager and agent for major jazz artists, and I bought a jazz club in NYC on my twenty-third birthday. A combination of bad luck and my burgeoning heroin addiction scuttled my music business career, and I fully descended into drugs until I read Kerouac's *On the Road* and became a voracious reader. A short time later, I had the epiphany that let me get clean, and started my recovery from addiction. I found my answers in books; reading was the catalyst for getting off drugs, and it gave me a framework for living out of the closet. I spent the first few years clean getting a degree in English from Columbia University with hopes of becoming a writer and worked at an AIDS hospice in gratitude for having somehow not gotten AIDS. My life was the opposite of what it had been when I was using drugs, and music wasn't a big part of it. Then for five years I'd worked the corporate job that had depleted my creativity and my interest in anything but making money.

I needed to catch up with what I'd missed. Betsy, who is ten years younger than me, turned me on to some new bands that I liked (Radiohead, Nine Inch Nails, Smashing Pumpkins), and I saw that a sea change had taken place in music. The hair bands, and homogenization of rock artists like David Bowie and Heart during the peak MTV years in the 1980s, had given way to grunge, hip hop, and metal. Artists like Nirvana, Eminem, and Metallica became huge and crossed over into the mainstream. Metal and hip hop artists were heavily tattooed, and that was where I wanted to find a band that embodied the outsider sensibility so deep in tattoo culture.

Rock bands like Nirvana, Rage Against the Machine, and Nine Inch Nails reminded me of the bands I'd grown up with; I knew that I would have lost my mind to them if those bands had arrived on the scene when I was a teenager. But the musical structure of some metal and hip hop was completely foreign to my ear. I needed a melody, and a chorus, and a bridge. Heavy metal bands like Metallica and Slayer just didn't move me, especially the fast, head-banging speed metal. I got the lyrics, and I knew what it was like to be alienated and on the fringes. I'd struggled with my sexuality growing up in the 1970s and lived a double life, and a lie, until I got off dope and came out as bisexual in my twenties—considered a cop-out at the time because you couldn't be two things. And being Jewish had always made me feel like an outsider—and marginalized, too. I had a foot in many worlds, but didn't entirely belong in any of them. I got what these bands were writing about. I felt I needed to experience what was going on at that moment, and not just read about it, to build a festival that was authentic. I put on my black jeans, a black T-shirt, a worn pair of Kenneth Cole half boots with the laces removed (inspired by Bernie Luther), and my Calvin Klein leather jacket. Like Colonel Kurtz from *Apocalypse Now*, who went airborne at thirty-eight with kids half his age, I was getting out of the boat, and heading into the mosh pit.

My first stop back in NYC was Sean's shop. It was great to see him, and to feed off his energy again as I told him about my new direction. He agreed I needed to pace myself and had news on some tattoo artists he had contacted. There was a kid in the shop, who overheard us talking and jumped right in, telling us the connections he had in the music business, and how he could get tickets for any show we wanted to see that night. The kid was in his early twenties, and it hit me that he typified the demographic of Tattoo the Earth's fans. He loved hip hop and rap metal, JNCO clothing, Jägermeister, MTV, and going to go concerts. He was practically hyperventilating, telling me everything he could do for me. Sean and I shot each other glances, and I told the kid to chill out, but the kid picked up his cell phone, got Sen Dog from Cypress Hill on the line, and started telling him about our project.

I'd heard of Cypress Hill, though I didn't know a lot about them, and I'd never heard of Sen Dog. But Sean was nodding his head, his glasses on the tip of his nose, indicating that the introduction was for real. Cypress Hill were part of that post-MTV emergence of hip hop, and were among the first California, Latino-influenced hip hop groups to have mainstream crossover. The group was founded by Sen Dog, B-Real, and DJ Muggs in LA in the late 1980s when they were teenagers, and by the mid-1990s they were one of the biggest bands in the world. They'd killed at Woodstock 1994 and headlined at Lollapalooza. I had a short chat with Sen Dog, who was receptive, and told him I'd send a pitch book and ring him next time I was in LA. I gave the kid a few pitch books and told him I'd get in touch after my trip to Austria. The kid was hyper, maybe well-connected, immediately committed to Tattoo the Earth, but he also seemed utterly and completely full of shit.

A few days later, Bernie had just about finished my sleeve at his shop in Vienna. Betsy and I visited some cool cemeteries and St.

Stephens Catacomb, with its basement walls of bones deposited during the great plague. Bernie agreed to do the tour; he was the first name tattooist to jump on board. The sleeve looked incredible, and I couldn't stop looking at it. He'd used white ink to outline a series of small triangles in the crook of my arm; the whole piece was completely unique. My tattoo made me feel like I had a bionic limb, and I held it awkwardly and stared at it, trying to get used to its power. Betsy liked it. She also liked the fact that I'd gotten tattooed on the road, so I'd leave ink and blood imprints on the hotel's sheets instead of on our own at home.

Back in NYC, the kid had flooded me with emails: B-Real from Cypress Hill wants to do the tour, and they're ready to meet us in LA. He wants to introduce me to potential sponsors and says members of Limp Bizkit and Staind are interested, and on and on. He wants us to go out to LA immediately, but I wasn't buying the kid a plane ticket based on one phone call. The kid acted hurt because I was skeptical and wondered what it would take to convince me he wasn't bullshitting. Sean had told me the Rolling Stones were playing in Philadelphia a few nights later, so I told the kid if he got me in to see the show, I'd buy him a ticket and we'd fly out to LA to see Cypress.

Next thing I know, I was watching the Stones in Philadelphia. The kid had done it, though when I saw the person who'd put us on the guest list, and asked him how he knew the kid, he said he didn't. He had never met him. He was actually not sure how we'd gotten added to the list, though he knew he'd authorized it. After the show, the kid admitted he'd pulled the Stones passes out of his ass and hadn't been sure they'd manifest until we were actually in the arena. The kid did have balls, and had earned a trip out to LA, even though he had also already shown himself to be pretty disgusting. He'd emptied the mini bar at the hotel after the concert in Philly, and when we spent a night at my house in Massachusetts before we flew west, he'd gotten profoundly drunk. Betsy looked at me like I was crazy, but I told her about Cypress Hill, and the Stones concert, and how he was my demographic.

"Well, your demographic is upstairs vomiting," she informed me. She spent most of the night hiding with her sister in the den while the kid blasted music and dry-heaved.

Our Chocolate Labrador puppy, Walter, was a total mush, like a teddy bear. He bit the kid; it was the first time we ever saw him even bare his teeth. Granted, we'd had Wally's balls removed a few days earlier, but it was still out of character. Betsy shook her head as the kid and I left for the airport, and told me she hoped it was worth it. I was having serious doubts about our trip. What the fuck was I doing with this idiot? But I had come this far with the kid and it was worth the risk. He had a fucked up family life, learning disabilities, and a giant chip on his shoulder. He'd been dismissed his entire life. But he loved music and the action, and he believed in my idea. I was following a path, he was on it, and it had been pretty entertaining so far. I relaxed and let go. I was in a scene from a dumb buddy movie, I told myself. The script had been written. I just needed to play my role.

I put the kid in a motel on the outskirts of LA and gave strict instructions to the staff to not under any circumstances let him charge anything to my credit card. I stayed in West Hollywood, and when I went back to the motel to pick him up he had a huge black eye. I didn't even want to know how it happened, and immediately felt a sense of dread and embarrassment. That first night we went by a radio station to see B-Real at his weekly radio show. He was cordial, wary, and busy, and said he hoped we could meet before I left. The kid also introduced me to Estevan Oriol, a photographer and music video director who was also Cypress's tour manager. Estevan and I ditched the kid and went to Mister Cartoon's tattoo shop, where Cartoon did a cool black and gray trippy skull thing on my shoulder above Bernie's tattoo. As I had done with Bernie, I just gave him the space on my arm, and he freehanded a design. Estevan and Cartoon were partners in a clothing line, and Cartoon was the tattoo artist of choice for Cypress Hill and many other rappers and athletes. They were taking West Coast Latino Lowrider culture to the mainstream.

The kid and I had dinner with Sen Dog at Benihana. It was becoming apparent at each meeting that the band only knew the kid peripherally and thought he was full of shit. In private, I told Sen Dog that I however was for real, and how I'd just met the kid, and that I'd like to come back out with Sean. The last night there, at the last minute, B-Real agreed to meet with us at a Korean barbecue restaurant off La Cienega, and he showed up with six members of his crew. The dinner was cordial and expensive. I gently pitched the show, and got an assurance we could meet again the next time I was in LA.

The kid had come through. By some miracle he'd pulled off the introduction, but now he had to be cut loose. He was too much of a liability and a deal breaker where Cypress was concerned; they wanted nothing to do with him. We had some laughs at the kid's expense. No one in the group could figure out how he'd gotten their phone numbers, or even how he'd gotten connected with them at all. The kid created a tornado of disinformation, and we had all been sucked up into it. I'd figure out how to compensate him later, but he was a problem and needed to be kept at a distance.

A few days after I got back from LA, I was off to Miami to meet with Jack Utsick, the independent promoter who music writer Bob Grossweiner had recommended I see. I'd sent a pitch book, and spoken to Naomi Fabricant, one of his staff. She was in charge of evaluating new proposals, and separated them into three piles; mine, she told me, was in the "look at now" pile. I could sense Naomi's enthusiasm over the phone. She thought Tattoo the Earth was forward thinking, and that tattooing was going to be huge, and she knew Jack would be interested in hearing more about it. When I met her I discovered that she was my age. She reminded me of the crazy

Jewish girls I tried to make out with at summer camp when I was a teenager.

Jack Utisck was a former airline pilot who had made a fortune bringing the hair replacement treatment Rogaine to the U.S. He would later go to prison for eighteen years when his business was exposed as a $200,000,000 fraud, but in 1999 he wanted to be in the music business but was having trouble breaking in. He had promoted some big shows but no tours or anything substantive. He was an outsider, and regardless of how much money he had, he wasn't allowed in the game.

I met with Jack at his penthouse in Miami, and as I walked into the main room to introduce myself to his lawyer, I almost stepped onto a gigantic antique mirror that was face up on the floor, being cleaned.

"Easy there," the lawyer said, as he grabbed my arm and pulled me back from the mirror, my foot an inch away from crashing into it. "It's a long way down."

"I bet it is," I replied.

Jack was enthusiastic, and said he wanted in, but that I still had a lot of work to do before he'd invest. I told him I was working on Cypress Hill and some other bands (Staind, Limp Bizkit), and that I would keep be in touch with Naomi and let him know when I got some commitments.

A few days later, Sean and I were in LA to meet with the Cypress crew without the kid, and we were starting to get somewhere. Sean and I were a force on the road, a byproduct of my having spent so much time getting tattooed by him. There's a synergy between an artist and client during a tattoo session, and Sean and I were forming a strong kinship. You sit there for hours, many times in various stages of undress, positioned in some weird manner under bright lights, and it hurts, and the machine buzzes and buzzes. If you look closely at a tattoo machine's needles puncturing the skin, it looks like oil rig pistons smashing the earth, except it's blood flying off and not dirt. You're in pain, and vulnerable, and it hurts more the longer it goes on. I was usually good for three hours before I started squirming, grabbing something with each touch of the machine, every muscle in my body tightening. You want to stop, but you won't because you're in deep with this other person and you want to cross the finish line with them. Sean could tell when I'd start to struggle. "Break, or keep going?" he'd ask, making sure to make eye contact. Or "Don't forget to breathe, Bro." You get that close and intimate with someone for so long, vulnerable for so long, you can't help but feel some love. You're in the trenches with this person, and he's an artist with a technical proficiency, but he's also your friend, shrink, priest, pimp, and adviser, whatever you need him to be to get through that tattoo. Now Sean was my partner and road buddy, and we were becoming an unstoppable force.

Sean and I had Easter dinner at Sen Dog's house; we had another dinner with B-Real and hung out in the studio. Sean and I had smoked a ton of pot in our lives, but whatever got passed to us in that studio rendered us almost mute. It felt like we were tripping. We somehow ended up at a compound in South Central LA with some tweaking cholos doing gas mask bong hits deep into the night. Now I was in a great buddy movie with Sean, and I couldn't wait to see what happened next.

Estevan and B-Real said I should come and hang out when they played in Hartford and Springfield, Massachusetts, and I did, and had a good time. I liked the music (it was the first hip hop I got into), and the stoner sensibility, and all the skulls in their branding. Then I flew to Indianapolis to see them, and that's when I started hanging out with DJ Muggs, the third founding member of Cypress. Muggs was from Queens, and we bonded over our shared New York roots. As DJ of the group, he chose the music to sample to go with the raps, and much of his choices were standards and rock music I listened to as a kid, like sampling Dusty Springfield's "Son of a Preacher Man" for the Cypress song "Hits from the Bong," or sampling Jimi

Hendrix for "How I Could Kill a Man."

A few weeks later, I went with Cypress Hill to Europe for a few festival dates in Austria and Germany. We spent a few days in Vienna, and like most bands on the road, they broke off into factions. B-Real was private, and guarded, and I didn't spend much time with him; Sen Dog was also off on his own. I pulled a couple of all-nighters with DJ Muggs and Estevan, smoking copious amounts of weed, bull-shitting, and sightseeing around Vienna. I took them to St. Stephens's catacombs, and they were blown away by the walls of compacted human bones. We visited another catacomb, and there were open coffins strewn about, and we were standing on ten feet of human bone. The plague must have been hell, we all agreed, and Estevan took some photos that would find their way onto the cover of their next album, *Skull & Bones*.

They were a good hang, and we were never at a loss for shit to talk about and had a lot of laughs. I'd rented a car, and though I was assured by Estevan that a parking space near the catacombs was legal, when we returned the car had been towed. Muggs and Estevan shot each other glances, like they were planning a getaway, and I told them they'd gotten me into this mess, and weren't going anywhere. We took a cab to the impound lot, and after a long wait, and a heaping dose of Germanic bureaucratic terrorism, we were told I needed my passport. I called a cab, and the lady in charge told us we couldn't wait inside. The three of us sat on the curb, and lay back onto the pavement. It was dark, it had started raining, and we hadn't slept in days. These guys are alright, I thought. They could have bailed, but they saw it through. When you hang sleepless with someone, and go on adventures together, you get a feel for them. We ultimately got the car back, and the next day the band took off in their bus for Germany, and I took the autobahn from Vienna to Nurburgring, smoking joints, drinking Red Bull, and driving 225 km/h with the radio cranked all the way up.

Rock Am Ring takes place at a Formula One racetrack and is one of two giant festivals taking place simultaneously in Germany in spring. There were five bands playing the main stage that year: Metallica headlined, and Cypress played before them. Cypress performed in front of 50,000 people, and then we hung out near the dressing room trailers waiting for Metallica to go on. We were told we could go up on stage and watch once the band got on stage, and there were a decent number of musicians waiting with us. It had been raining and the grounds were muddy, and as Metallica made their way to the stage, we saw their drummer, Lars Ulrich, being carried piggy back by a roadie through the grounds, and up the stairs of the stage.

"You know, I'm a rock star," B-Real said, shaking his head. "And I'd never do that shit."

"Just so you know, don't think I'm carrying any of you motherfuckers," Estevan declared to the band.

Metallica were the real deal, a full-on stadium band, and though I'd never been a fan, I got sucked in immediately. It was a melodic assault, mighty and foreboding, and you didn't need to be into them to appreciate it. The power, the connection with the fans, and the authenticity; it was inspiring to see it all from the stage. I stood next to Lars's drums (and his clean sneakers), and the guy was like a machine. I looked out over 50,000 people, and closed my eyes. I leaned over to Muggs and Estavan.

"Metallica's going to play my New York Tattoo the Earth show," I told them. "It's a done deal."

When I got back home, B-Real said that Cypress was in, and told me to send a letter of interest to their agent. A few days later I was watching MTV, and they had a news clip with B-Real talking about a new Cypress album, and how the band was going to be doing Tattoo the Earth. I went down to Miami to meet with Jack Utsick and Naomi, and we decided to send out offer letters to Kid Rock, Red Hot Chili Peppers, Orgy, and Everlast, with an offer for a 1999 fall tour. The offer letters were rejected pretty quickly, and then

Cypress's agent indicated the band might not be available. B-Real started hedging, told me to be patient, and all the momentum stopped.

What the fuck? I'd gotten a band and someone to put up the money, and I was dead in the water. That's how I learned that one of the reasons it was difficult for outsiders to get real access to talent was because it often didn't matter what the bands wanted. The live music business seems like a vast, complicated enterprise, but it is controlled by relatively few people. At any given time, in any given genre, there are a small number of artists that can sell out a stadium, arena, or amphitheater (if they're even planning to tour), and they are controlled by a handful of agents. Jack Utsick had millions of dollars to invest, but it didn't matter; they only allowed him to nibble at the edges. A full tour with a level of talent like ours was off the table. Agents and managers were the key, but I was nowhere close to finding one. No agent I had spoken to had shown much enthusiasm, and I was struggling with what my next steps might be to keep the thing alive.

I was still undeterred, for the most part. But I was physically run down from non-stop traveling and too much alcohol and debauching. I was getting tattooed regularly on the road, so I was constantly sore and healing, and I started losing weight, and having terrible stomach problems. I'd had Hepatitis C for thirteen years, and though I never had any symptoms, I shouldn't have been drinking. I tried to limit myself to just smoking pot all day, but it was hard not to do other things on the road.

I was getting so thin I looked like I was dying. The first doctor I saw in my small town in Massachusetts told me, without giving me any tests, that I probably had liver cancer. I thought I was a goner. I'd been obsessed with death as kid, and it had shaped my sensibility. I was smack dab in the middle of several high risk groups for AIDS in NYC in the 1980s, and somehow survived, when most everyone didn't. Many of the people I got clean with in Narcotics Anonymous died, and after working at the AIDS hospice I always felt like a ghostly survivor living on borrowed time. And then I watched as my parents died early, and badly, and screaming from cancer, so dying young seemed to make sense. Frankly, I was surprised to even be alive at all. And the irony didn't escape me. I knew I was getting close with Tattoo the Earth, and I still believed it could be big, and now I was going to be like Jonathan Larson with *Rent* and die right before my dream came true.

But I wasn't going out afraid and screaming. Though I had been a wussy my whole life when it came to my own pain, all the death and suffering I'd seen pushed me to withstand as much punishment as possible. I'd get tattooed for four hours, have a steak, get my nipple pierced, then go play in a dungeon, then go out all night, and then finish the tattoo for a couple of hours the next day. I'd never had any interest in testing the limits of my own pain tolerance before, but something had changed in the past year, especially after my mother died, and I guess I needed to know that I could withstand any horror that might attack my body.

After several more alarmist doctors (one thought I had Crohn's Disease), I found a surgeon I trusted in Manhattan who told me I had gallstones, and that I needed to have my gallbladder removed. Turns out I'd gotten the parasite Giardia from the well water at my house, and it had ravaged my innards. My liver and everything else were okay, and the surgery went fine, but I was weak and shaken, and running out of ideas.

"I sacrificed an organ for the rock & ink tour," I told Sean, "But it will take more than that to stop me."

"The darkness drops again; but now I know that twenty centuries of stony sleep were vexed to nightmare by a rocking cradle…" – W.B. Yeats

Jeff Hanneman (Slayer)

Ruyter Suys (Nashville Pussy)
Photo by Soren McCarty

Scott Alderman and Betsy Sparrow

Sean Vasquez

Corey Taylor (Slipknot)

Bernie Luther

Lajon Witherspoon (Sevendust) and Filip Leu

Shawn Crahan (Slipknot)

Paul Booth

Kerry King (Slayer)

Scott Alderman

Filip Leu

52

Titine Leu

Shannon Larkin (Amen)

Fran Strine

Chapter Four

Rescue Squads

My gallbladder was the second non-essential organ I'd lost in the past few years—my appendix went first—and I felt more mortal knowing I was half a lung and a kidney from being in deep shit. The surgery was successful, I felt better immediately, and I started to put some weight back on. I wasn't sure how much more I could do for Tattoo the Earth, or if it would even make a difference. Sean, Betsy, and I had dinner, and I asked them what they thought we should do next, and their response was a resounding "How should we know?" I had been driving the project since the start, with clear vision and purpose, and no one ever doubted my strategy. But I was starting to doubt it, and doubt myself and the idea, and I felt totally alone.

When things had started heating up with Cypress Hill, a friend referred me to Stewart Levy, an entertainment attorney in NYC. Stewart represented Queen Latifah, and had at one time represented Tupac Shakur. Stewart got a kick out of the Tattoo the Earth concept, and for him, the tour was the least interesting thing in the pitch book. It was all the spinoffs that turned him on. I liked Stewart immediately and decided to use him for any agreements I might need with Cypress and Jack Utsick. He had provided good counsel as I sent out letters of interest to the bands and tried to get a tour off the ground. Now he confirmed for me that Cypress's agent was playing games, and he had concerns about Utsick, and he said I should pull back and regroup. He was impressed I had gotten as far as I had on my own, and said he knew someone who could be the final piece in my puzzle.

Stewart introduced me to Paul Zukoski, a producer of lifestyle-themed tours like Jazz Explosion and Solid Gold Dance Party; and of package tours like A Walk Down Abbey Road, a tribute to the Beatles featuring Ann Wilson, John Entwistle, and Todd Rundgren. Zukoski had produced the B.B. King Blues Festival for the previous ten years, and that had made him some serious money. He had a young second wife, two small children, and a huge house in New Jersey. He told me he thought Tattoo the Earth was the best tour idea he'd ever heard.

Zukoski had come up the hard way, and climbed and clawed to get his success, and had a decent sized chip on his shoulder. He was ten years older than me, so meeting him was like seeing the ghost of my shoulder-chip future. Zukoski could make money off anything. He told me about an early hustle selling lottery tickets at worksites.

"Rescue squads," he told me, "were where the real money was."

Zukoski knew about tours. He was the first one who broke it down for me: how the talent is controlled, how each entity makes their money, how you control costs on the road; all of it down to the nitty gritty. He said the reason Cypress's agent had bailed on us was because the band wasn't big enough to headline an amphitheatre or arena show, and the agent would never put them in a position to have an unsuccessful tour, regardless of the money. He chuckled as I told him my exploits with Azoff, Lyle, and the rest, and in speaking with him I realized that while I had some of the pieces required to bring the tour to life, Zukoski knew which ones were still missing and could put it all together. A festival tour producer puts together a package that includes the bands, crew, staging, lights, and sound, travel expenses, touring entourage, etc., and then sells that package to promoters around the country with the producer's profit built in, plus there is T-shirt, vendor, and sponsor money. How a producer manages expenses on the road was key to a profitable tour, and that's where Zukoski excelled. We soon had a deal to become partners.

He said agents don't even think about next summer's tours until the end of the year, and then after the New Year they jockey around until February, and then announce the summer line-ups. Zukoski did business with all the major agencies, and the plan was to set up meetings in LA with them after Thanksgiving. In the meantime, he would work the phones to see what bands were planning to tour in 2000. He told me I could stop running around like a lunatic, and could relax, heal up, and get ready for the LA meetings. But it was hard to sit still. Until I met Zukoski, if I stopped, then Tattoo the Earth stopped; I was the only one driving it. Ideas are fragile things that need to be nurtured, and to be constantly pushed forward, even if in the wrong direction. Zukoski was driving now, and though I had faith in his ability to succeed, it was hard to just chill without feeling like the whole thing was dying. I needed to keep busy, so I decided to "wag the dog" a little, and create some buzz for the brand.

The vomiting demographic had introduced me to a singer in Huntington Beach named Lauren Boquette, and Lauren and I connected during one of my Cypress trips. He was the front man in a moderately successful industrial band called Drown and was completely wired into the LA hard music scene. He was soon committed to making the project happen, and we came up with some guerilla marketing to get the Tattoo the Earth brand in front of fans. Lauren put together a street crew around the country that distributed our post cards at events. We handed them out at the inaugural Coachella festival, though we originally wanted a booth and were told that tattooing didn't jibe with the Coachella aesthetic. We sent a street team to a big radio show in Philadelphia, and to the

Las Vegas Metal Festival. Lauren and his team handed out 50,000 cards at Woodstock '99, and even got called out in *Rolling Stone* for driving a van right into the rave and tossing out Tattoo the Earth swag. Lauren not only helped build a national street team, he also gave Zukoski and me the latest information on which bands were hot, and which ones were about to get hot. He was preparing a list in advance of our LA meetings in November and became our biggest cheerleader and advocate.

K Rock, the big rock station at the time in New York City, held an annual event at Jones Beach called the Dysfunctional Family Picnic, and I spent $5,000 for a booth there to promote the tour plus more to fly Naomi from Jack Utsick's office in from Miami and hire a crew. The night before we all stayed at a crappy motel that was under construction and didn't see until morning that there were giant dirt piles all around it. Having the crew together for the first time was inspiring, and we took a picture holding a Tattoo the Earth banner in front of one of the dirt piles.

"This is how new ideas happen," I told them, standing atop the dirt pile. "A group of people believe in something, and throw themselves fully into it to make it real. All ideas are like that. It's a person like you or me. Ages ago someone got frustrated because the flat roof on their house kept caving in after it rained, and came up with an idea to angle two sections so the rain slid off. There was nothing magical about it. It was born out of a desire to keep their family dry. Our idea is born out of a desire to tattoo the entire fucking earth, and that campaign officially begins today."

Once we were set up at Jones Beach, Sean and his partner did a tattoo demonstration (we couldn't get a permit to tattoo the public), we sold some T-shirts, and held a raffle for tickets to an undefined NYC show. After setting up, Naomi and I stood looking at the booth, and I asked her what she thought.

"You're having a raffle for tickets to a New York show that doesn't exist, that's part of a tour that barely has any prospects," she replied. "I think it's awesome."

In addition to building the brand, I also worked on recruiting tattoo artists. Sean and I went to Amsterdam at the end of August to meet with Henk Schiffmacher, aka Hanky Panky, one of the top tattoo artists in the world and a legendary character. Henk was tickled when I told him how my first tattoo was from his tribal design page in *Modern Primitives*, though he chastised me for cutting the design out of the book. He had recently retired from his shop, and was devoting his time and efforts to the Tattoo Museum he had recently opened. Henk traveled the world, and was one of the key players preserving the history of tattoo, and legitimizing it as an art form.

"A tattoo is like a stamp in a passport," he told me. "It lets people know where you've been, and gives them an idea of who you are."

Henk had tattooed members of the Red Hot Chili Peppers, Pearl Jam, and Kurt Cobain, and developed a reputation as a premier rock & roll tattoo artist. He was a historian, raconteur, fine artist, curator, and a bit of a maniac. He and Anthony Kiedis from Red Hot Chili Peppers had taken an infamous trip to Borneo together, where they had to be rescued by record company helicopter after their Bornean guides abandoned them because of their prima donna rock star behavior. Henk was a fascinating guy, and brilliant, and there was no topic on which he wasn't erudite and engaging. His passion was his museum, which was filled with a lifetime of collecting tattoo artifacts and culture; he told me that the museum's website was getting more hits than Anne Frank. He tattooed a tribal piece on my upper back that took about forty-five minutes, and said he liked the Tattoo the Earth concept, and agreed to be part of it.

The night I got back from Amsterdam, I went to a show at CBGB in New York City, ended up getting wasted drunk, and did cocaine for the first time in fourteen years. And though I had a good time roaring into the night, the next day I felt cadaverous, my organs moaning and creaking like plumbing in an old house. I wasn't sure if I would survive the drive back to Massachusetts. I stopped at a rest stop to get Advil, Tums, and a Yoo-hoo—and to go the bathroom. I was peeing at a urinal when I became 96% sure that I'd shitted myself; it felt like all matter in my body had deposited itself in my pants. It was crowded. Every urinal was occupied, and all the doors on the stalls were closed. I stood in the middle of the bathroom and prayed for death. I was so tired and plum out of ideas; I thought I was going to start crying. Then I felt someone touch my arm, and looked to my right and saw a kid, maybe seven years old, holding the hand of his brother who was a few years younger.

"Go in that one," he said, motioning toward one of the stalls that had a door ajar.

Our eyes locked, and his were preternaturally deep and wise, Buddha-like, and he nodded and motioned to the stall again. I thanked him, bowing with clasped hands, and went in and cleaned myself up. The encounter reminded me that I was on a mystical journey, and I needed to keep my eyes open because the messenger could be anyone and could appear anywhere.

The encounter should have reminded me that I was a fucking addict with Hepatitis C, and I had just done coke, of all things, and drunk myself into a stupor. I'd given up coke after being a speed freak in my teens, and alcohol had never been my thing, and I was surprised I'd done both to excess. My health aside, I was pushing the boundaries of my addiction, though I never felt like I was danger of being addicted to anything. I knew when I'd kicked my last heroin habit cold turkey in 1987 that I would never shoot heroin again, but I never thought I would not use again. Ten clean years later, sitting in a car outside Memorial Sloan-Kettering as one of my oldest friends was dying, I'd smoked a joint with her husband and another friend; both had been cleaner than me. I could make excuses that I was in pain, and anxious about family and business, but the reality is I wanted to smoke a joint and I did. And once the initial shock and guilt wore off, I loved being stoned. I'd missed smoking pot just about every day I was clean and sober, and it made me feel like I was normal again.

It was all fine at first, but then I started drinking, and dabbled with some Percocets after a dental procedure. The other two friends I relapsed with went back to an active heroin addiction (one of them died not long ago of liver failure). But I never felt like that was even a possibility for me. I smoked pot from morning to night, and combined with anti-depressents, it made me feel balanced. But now I had done coke, and shit myself in a rest stop, and I knew I had pushed myself too far. I was wracked with anxiety about Tattoo the Earth, but worse was that Betsy's mother wasn't doing well, and it was becoming a possibility that she might not make it. It made everything feel hopeless, and I was full of rage and resentment.

Betsy and I needed to get away, so we took a three-week, cross-country trip to Yellowstone. For the first time since I'd started Tattoo the Earth I actually turned it off for a while, and we both had a great time—a legendary time, and we marveled at all the shit we had been through, and that we were still good together, just the two of us with no distractions. We planned a trip to New Orleans for Halloween weekend (we thought it might become an annual tradition). Then I got into an argument outside the airport during our changeover in Memphis, said something stupid to the wrong person, and got myself arrested. I was taken from the airport to a police station in Memphis that was crowded with newly hauled in reprobates, and by late afternoon it was clear I was staying overnight, and that since it was Friday, I'd most likely be there until Monday. Every part of the police station had people sleeping in it, and I rolled up my leather jacket as a pillow, and slept in a hallway. I heard horror stories about how long it can take to get processed (one guy had been there a week), and I started to freak. Just before dawn, I saw the two clerks who worked in the office getting ready to finish up their shift, and I walked over to them.

"Hey guys," I said, leaning on the desk. "How much will it take to get me out of here right now?"

They looked at each other and paused for a moment.

"Five hundred," one of them said. "Two-fifty each."

"Done," I said, slapping the desk. "Let's get the fuck out of here."

Fifteen minutes later the three of us walked out of the jail, drove to a bank machine, and I gave them their money. I also gave them Tattoo the Earth postcards, and told them to contact me if we did a Memphis show, and I'd hook them up with passes (I had also given cards to all the prisoners).

While I was in jail, Betsy was sitting in a shitty motel working with our lawyer to get me out. She was pissed, and refused to get on another plane with me to go home, so we rented a car and drove back to Massachusetts. I felt terrible. I joked that she'd known I was crazy before she married me, but she wasn't laughing. She was stressed about her mother. Betsy was the oldest of four kids, and had a sister who was still in high school. Her father died at 42 when she was in college, and the family had barely recovered from that. She and I had been through so much together, and she knew I'd be there for her mother, but I could tell she was losing patience with my insanity.

But she lightened up as we drove. I bought her a license plate at a truck stop that said, "My Next Husband will Be Normal," and took a picture of her with it looking forlorn and forgiving at the camera. Now that I was out of jail, I was able to find a lawyer in Mississippi who made the whole thing go away; I never even had to go back for a court date. And now it was time to stay put in Massachusetts and prepare for the agent meetings.

Zukoski and I were going to be in LA for five days, the first two hanging out and getting in sync, the last three in non-stop meetings with agents. We took some long drives, and he showed me the house in the Hollywood Hills he'd been living in during the 1994 earthquake. Our first meeting was with a smaller agency that had some decent punk and hardcore bands. But Zukoski told me we weren't just buying talent, we were looking for an agent to represent the tour, and that this agent wasn't big enough to do it.

"I set this first meeting so we can get comfortable selling together, and to give you an idea of what to expect," he told me. "This agent, the first thing he's going to tell us is why it won't work. Why is he saying that? Because it wasn't his idea. Agents don't get many ideas, and they're resentful when someone else shows up with one, let alone a great one."

At that first meeting, after some pleasantries, the agent took some time to look through the pitch book.

"I like the idea," he began, "but let me tell you why it won't work."

We met with a few other smaller agencies, but we were there primarily to meet with CAA and William Morris, and of the two, Zukoski had his sights on CAA. The biggest agency in the world, CAA represented Ozzy Osbourne's annual tour, Ozzfest, and Warped Tour, the annual punk rock tour, and Zukoski felt they would be the best agency for us. Zukoski had been buying blues, jazz, and oldies artists for his tours from the agent we were meeting with for years, and they had developed a good relationship. Zukoski thought the agent would see this tour as a way to broaden his roster and his profile within the agency. As we sat in the CAA lobby waiting for someone to bring us up, I couldn't stop staring at the biggest Roy Lichtenstein painting I'd ever seen up close.

"These folks aren't messing around," Zukoski said when he noticed I was paying attention to the painting and not him.

The agent got the concept. He sat there twirling his eyebrows as he read the pitch book, and came to the realization that Zukoski hoped he would have. We talked about what bands anchor the tour, and the agent said Green Day should do it. He took us immediately down the hall through a maze of offices to meet Green Day's agent, who loved the idea, and started talking about time frames when Green Day might be available and what other groups might work with the show. Zukoski and I were terrific together, and I gave my best pitch yet. At one point, I pretended to be using a jackhammer, bouncing around the floor to demonstrate our goal of literally tattooing the earth.

Back in the first agent's office, he told us that our tour was exactly what he had been looking for, and that he would call us in a few days to generate a deal memo. Zukoski and I stood on the sidewalk outside the building looking at each other like we'd seen a ghost, or had been deposited into an alternate reality.

"Did that just happen?" I asked him.

"I think it did," he replied, "It's not supposed to happen like that, but sometimes it does, and it just did."

I thought about the past year since I'd met with Irving Azoff. I'd been to over 150 shows all over the U.S. and Europe, stayed 200 nights in hotels, flown 50,000 miles, and invested a lot of money. I lost an organ, got busted, and now here I was with Zukoski, and the meeting I always imagined would happen had just actually happened. We stood there stunned for a while, and the rest of the meetings were a blur. William Morris expressed interest, but Zukoski was focused on reeling in CAA. A few days after we returned, they called and told us we'd have a deal memo within 24 hours.

And then we heard nothing. For days, and then for a week. Zukoski worked the phones to find out what was going wrong. He spoke to the agent, but they were stalling us. It seemed that when the subject of Tattoo the Earth was brought up at a staff meeting, the agents for Ozzfest and Warped Tour were dead set against it. They were already fighting for talent, and another summer tour would weaken the existing ones. The Lollapalooza festival in the nineties had opened the floodgates, and there were an increasing number of lifestyle festivals competing for fans and talent. Warped Tour had been founded in 1995 by Kevin Lyman and could feature up to 50 punk and pop bands in alternative venues. It had a low budget (planks of wood laid out between two open trucks would serve as a stage), big sponsors, skater sensibility, and it had become a launching pad for up-and-coming bands. Ozzfest, the metal tour created by Sharon Osbourne, Ozzy Osbourne's wife, was then in its infancy, and took place in more traditional venues, anchored by Ozzy, and sometimes, Black Sabbath. When Kevin Lyman and Sharon Osbourne found out about Tattoo the Earth, which could syphon bands off from both tours, they let their voices be heard. We were put on the back burner. We told the agent at CAA it didn't need to be a summer tour, and that we could do a winter arena tour, but we were met with silence.

Zukoski wasn't happy. Though there was a small chance we might still have a deal with CAA, once Ozzfest and Warped Tour finalized their line-ups, Zukoski didn't want scraps, and he didn't like getting dicked around. We met with Lauren Boquette, our guerilla marketing guru, while we were in LA, and Lauren told us that we should go after Slipknot, who were tearing up the metal world, and whose debut album had just gone platinum. Lauren thought the first tour should be renegade, with the hottest, hardest new bands. He thought a huge band like Metallica or the Chili Peppers, though incredible to have headline (we should be so lucky), wouldn't allow us to establish our brand, and that we would get swallowed up. We could soften and mainstream the tour in the future if we wanted, but the first year should be dangerous, and feel uncertain, like the future. He believed Slipknot was the band that could make that happen.

A few weeks into CAA's silent treatment, Zukoski set up a meeting with Agency Group in New York. Zukoski had a long history of buying talent from them and was close to the managing director. Most importantly, they represented Slipknot, and we were meeting them with one band in mind.

Chapter Five

Clown's Blessing

At the end of 1999, Steve Richards, Slipknot's manager, and Sharon Osbourne, the wife of Ozzy Osbourne and producer of Ozzfest, had lunch in Los Angeles and agreed that Slipknot would headline the second stage on Ozzfest 2000. They shook on it. Sharon Osbourne had already become one of the biggest players in music by then and was known to be ruthless. She had resuscitated Ozzy's career in the 1980s after he got fired from Black Sabbath, stealing him from her own father's management company. Sharon's father Don Arden was a legend in the music business in England (he managed Little Richard, Small Faces, and Black Sabbath) and was known to be a cutthroat character. But Sharon took him on, and Ozzy's solo career and Ozzfest were proof of her skill in developing talent. She would become even bigger—a household name—a few years down the road with reality shows like *The Osbournes, America's Got Talent, The X Factor,* and her talk show, *The Talk.* But back in 1999, Ozzfest was still establishing itself, and securing Slipknot to headline the second stage was a key part of her plans. Slipknot had been the breakout stars of the previous Ozzfest, and had rocketed from obscurity to stardom.

When we met with Steve Martin, the managing director of Agency Group, he told us about Slipknot and Ozzfest, but said he didn't think it was a done deal; at least contracts hadn't been signed yet. Steve Martin and Dave Kirby, the Agency Group agent representing Slipknot, did not get along. Slipknot was Kirby's first big act, and Martin thought Kirby was too wrapped up in the band, and had forgotten who he really worked for. Touring and recording artists are a tightly controlled commodity, and everyone is jockeying for a financial piece, and their bit of control. Typically, an established artist has a manager who oversees the entire enterprise; an agent who is responsible for booking live appearances, and a public relations firm for publicity and image control. Then there is a merchandiser who handles all the T-shirts and swag, a record company A&R person who coordinates recordings, a person who produces their recordings, a road manager, a road crew, and on and on. Established bands effectively have a moat around them. But Slipknot's rise had been fast—a few years earlier they were unknowns travelling in a van; now they had a debut album that had sold a million copies—and everyone was fighting for a piece of them. Their moat was still being dug and hadn't been filled with water.

Steve Martin said the band's manager, Steve Richards, was prone to changing his mind and that it would be worth it to approach him. As a courtesy, we first met with Slipknot's agent Dave Kirby, who was cold as ice and pissed he even had to see us. I couldn't blame him. He'd finally gotten his first big breakout band, and new stature with Sharon Osbourne and Ozzfest, and now we'd come along wanting to throw a wrench in the works. Kirby was firmly against it, and established a roadblock to the band. Steve Martin suggested we do an end run around it and go directly to the band. Zukoski told me that this was highly unusual, and he posited that the rift between Martin and Kirby was deep, and Martin wanted to exert more control over Slipknot.

Slipknot were playing in Washington, DC, at the end of January, and their manager would be there, so we made a plan to go, but first we headed to New York to see Henk Schiffmacher's lecture at the American Museum of Natural History's tattoo exhibition in New York, the first major exhibition featuring body art by a top museum. The exhibition was called "Body Art: Marks of Identity," and featured the art and anthropology of body modification, with a focus on paintings, books, history, and body art itself. They presented artifacts dating back thousands of years as well as the first book to ever mention body art, *Anthropometamorphosis: Man Transform'd: or, the Artificiall Changling*, which was published in 1650. Sean Vasquez had helped arrange some of the artist panels, and we were both featured in the short film that accompanied the exhibit. Henk's lecture was well received, and his knowledge of tattoo origins on each continent was impressive. For example, as soon as ancient people formed civilizations they had begun to decorate and modify their bodies, and Henk's descriptions were vivid and illuminating. There was a party for Henk at Sean's shop afterwards, and Zukoski and Henk got a chance to meet. We filled Henk in on what's going on with Slipknot, and he agreed to come with us to DC to see the band.

The drive down to DC was a lot of laughs, and a real education for Zukoski about tattoo culture, tattoo artists, and the challenges we were facing working with them. Zukoski noted that tattoo artists, unlike successful musicians or fine artists, have no management. We laughed at how insane the music business would be if the musicians didn't have management (as if it wasn't insane enough). We stopped at what turned out to be an Ethiopian-owned Italian restaurant in Maryland with incredible chicken parmigiana, which we took as a good omen. Slipknot were playing at the 500-seat DC venue 9:30 Club, and they were insane: nine of them in matching numbered jumpsuits and creepy horror masks, like the most demented marching band ever. I'd never seen or heard anything like it, and I'd seen and heard some shit. Henk said the same thing, and thought it ironic that I was planning a show on body art while the band I wanted to sign wore jumpsuits that covered every inch of exposed flesh. My original idea had been a mainstream Woodstock-vibed celebration of body art; if Slipknot headlined Tattoo the Earth, it would be like Satan's house band playing the apocalypse. And that was cool. I learned early on that it didn't matter what I wanted. It was about what the kids wanted, and from my field work going to concerts I discovered that the kids wanted to feel like they belonged to something, and they wanted cool shit. Zukoski didn't know what to make of the band; he thought they were a gimmick. But I thought there was more to it. Slipknot didn't move me, but I respected the devotion their fans had for the band, and vice versa, and the craft and alchemy that went into making something so chaotic and affecting.

Slipknot's manager Steve Richards was expecting us, and we spoke with him right after the show. He was in his early thirties and had the same hustler energy as the vomiting demographic. He and Zukoski had both grown up in the DC area, and had much in common. Richards's father was a local DJ, and he and Zukoski had done some shows together in Maryland in the 1980s. When he and Paul finished chatting, he called his father and a few minutes later came bounding back over to us.

"My father said you're a stand-up guy," Richards said enthusiastically. "He said you're a person I should be in business with, and we should talk seriously about Tattoo the Earth."

He took all of us onto the tour bus, where Henk held court with the band. He took a look at their tattoos and talked about the ancient history of masks in entertainment and culture. Unmasked and out of costume they were all young sweaty midwestern guys finishing the night's work and were welcoming and approachable. Richards said we should send him an offer, and a few days later we did, doubling what Ozzfest had offered. Then nothing happened. I kept an organizer during that time, and for much of February and March, many days had only "Clusterfuck" written in. I was in the midst of my seasonal depression, and Dave Kirby was stalling, and the longer he stalled the better chance he stood of riding out our offer. Finally Zukoski pushed the issue, and we had a lunch with Richards and Kirby. Richards said he wanted to do the tour, and wanted to bring it to the band as an alternative to Ozzfest. Kirby had done everything he could to stop us, but he could only block us for so long before Richards would get pissed off.

The next day Zukoski spoke to Slipknot's leader, Shawn Crahan—also known by the name of his stage personae, "Clown"—and he gave us his blessing. He told Zukoski that Slipknot had never taken a traditional path and that the renegade spirit of our tour made sense for them. He also said to Zukoski what he would say to me later on: "My manager made all of this happen, and I do what my manager tells me to do." A week later, I was in LA to meet with Richards and his publicist, and a week after that there was an article in the *Los Angeles Times* and *Boston Globe* announcing that Slipknot was doing Tattoo the Earth, followed by coverage on MTV.

I had been averaging twenty or so visitors to the Tattoo the Earth website each day; after the announcements we started getting 100,000 a day. It was fucking righteous to see Tattoo the Earth come to life. On a conference call with Richards, Kirby, and Clown, we discussed the other bands we wanted to do the tour. One concern, and a valid one, was that Slipknot had never headlined an arena tour. They had barely graduated from clubs to theaters let alone anchored a summer festival, and we agreed we needed a strong co-headliner. We sent out letters of interest to all the other agencies, and put offers to Metallica and Rage Against the Machine. Both declined. Zukoski felt that if we didn't get a strong co-headliner, Kirby would be able to convince Richards that our show was too risky, and he'd bail and go back to Ozzfest.

Needless to say, Sharon Osbourne was pissed. She'd lost her

second stage headliner, a band with a lot of buzz as well as several of the new, hot bands that were planning to jump ship to be on our tour with Slipknot. Richards had shaken her hand, and he'd fucked her over, and she was having none of it. Zukoski knew Kirby was keeping a channel of communication open with Sharon, but Richards was holding firm with us. We put an offer to Slayer, one of the original thrash metal bands to come up in the eighties (Metallica, Megadeth, Anthrax, and Slayer are considered the cornerstone of hard metal). They were a band with a loyal following, and a strong touring history, and we wanted them to co-headline the main stage. We also put offers in to the Brazilian band, Sepultura, another of the older hard metal bands, and Coal Chamber, a Goth band that had recently released a well-received second album. We were starting to move quickly.

Just as we were getting ready to announce some bands, Steve Richards got a brain tumor. I truly felt bad for Richards, but I also knew we were fucked. Zukoski knew it too. Zukoski had been speaking to Richards constantly, and now Richards had had brain surgery, and was completely off the radar. Richards rented a house in Malibu to convalesce, and Zukoski decided to move out there for a few weeks to help with his recovery, stay close to him, and keep him connected to Tattoo the Earth. As Richards started to improve, he and Zukoski formed a strong bond. Zukoski liked him, and even though Richards had a reputation for being unreliable, Zukoski also felt he could trust him.

We announced Slayer, Sepultura, and Coal Chamber, and then we found out Metallica wanted to partner for a show at Giants Stadium. They were headlining their own summer tour, but the support bands on the tour, including Korn and Kid Rock, were not available to do the New York show. Metallica were not quite big enough to carry Giants Stadium by themselves anymore, and the idea was to combine Metallica with our show. It was major development for us, but it was almost June, our first show was July

15, and we hadn't announced any dates or put tickets on sale. When we finally put the thirty-eight dates on our website, and made it official, Sharon Osbourne became even more livid. Half of our dates were in Clear Channel venues, and Ozzfest was in business with them. Clear Channel and its ancestors had changed live music by purchasing the majority of venues across the US—arenas, amphitheaters and concert halls—and used that leverage to break the competition. Before Clear Channel, there had been multiple promoters in all the major markets, and for the most part the venues were open to anyone. Once Clear Channel had all the venues, they could make deals with artists that independent promoters and local venues could not. They could offer, say, Dave Matthews or Bruce Springsteen all the proceeds from their own ticket sales and still make a fortune on T-shirts, parking, and beer. If you didn't own a venue, there was no way to compete, and that killed off most of the independent promoters. They also owned hundreds of thousands of billboards, and thousands of radio stations, and kept our bands off their radio stations, and that hurt in some markets (the promoter of our Red Rocks show would later sue Clear Channel for keeping our bands off the radio). They were everywhere, and owned everything.

In short order, Sharon Osbourne got Clear Channel to rescind all our dates except for one: a parking lot in Detroit. We felt lucky to still have the eighteen remaining shows, though the routing looked like it was done by a drunk throwing darts at a map. Days off between shows on a tour kill you financially, and now we had holes in the schedule that couldn't be filled. I ran into Kevin Lyman, founder of Warped Tour, at a show, and he wasn't happy.

"What the hell are you doing?" he asked me. "You just dropped your tour on top of me, and now I've got you playing right before or after my dates."

"What am I supposed to do? Sit it out? I asked him. "We tried to sell this to CAA, and if they had bought it we wouldn't be having this discussion right now."

He wasn't having it, and he wasn't wrong. There were several markets where Tattoo the Earth, Ozzfest, and Warped Tour played on successive nights, and that wasn't good for anyone. Most of the dates Clear Channel had pulled were amphitheaters, and since they owned the majority of them, we were left with eighteen shows in alternative venues like rodeos, parking lots, parks, and racetracks. Plus, we were starting out on the West Coast, but we had to get back east for the Giants Stadium show in five days and could only fit in one show before heading back west where we would finish up in California. It was a mess and cost us a lot, but the Metallica show was worth it just for the cachet. I fell to my knees in tears when I heard Howard Stern announce that Metallica were going to Tattoo the Earth at Giants Stadium on July 20, 2000; and it was surreal hearing the ad spot I wrote promoting the Boston show on the radio: "This crusade is going to leave its mark [sound of buzzing tattoo machines]. Ouch! Tattoo the Earth!"

Sean was at Coney Island one day and saw a plane pulling a banner that read "Metallica Tattoos the Earth."

"Fucking, Scott!" he screamed as the plane flew by.

The tour's routing may have been a disaster, but we were officially on the map, and now we had to go into overdrive to promote the shows. Ozzfest announced their dates in March. We announced ours in in the middle of June, and still didn't have all the dates locked in, or a firm main stage line-up. The second stage bands were already set because the record companies paid to have their band on the tour, as was standard practice for festivals and tours. It was an effective way for a record company to get a new band exposure, and they considered it a marketing expense. For us, it helped defray the cost of having to overpay for all of the main stage bands, an unavoidable cost of doing business for a debut tour.

One day, Zukoski said he had a call set up with a record executive who wanted to get his band, Systematic, on the second stage, and Zukoski asked if I'd like to join him on the call.

"Listen, Lars," Zukoski started off, after introducing me, "I appreciate your enthusiasm for Tattoo the Earth, but our line-up is set. These shows are only so many hours long, and if I could fit your band in, believe me I would. There just isn't room."

As soon as Lars started speaking, I realized it was Lars Ulrich, Metallica's drummer, and that Systematic was on his record label. Zukoski had no idea who Lars was, and I had no way to get in touch with Zukoski (texting wasn't a thing back then) and didn't want to interrupt. I just listened as he basically told Lars to take a hike.

"Are you going to be at the Giants Stadium show?" Zukoski asked him.

"Uh, yeah," Lars replied haltingly.

"Why don't you come by and introduce yourself at the show, and we can talk about getting your band on for next year."

Zukoski couldn't believe it when I phoned him after the call, and thought he blew it, but I thought it was effective. Lars must have thought Zukoski was so badass he didn't care what the headliner wanted. Systematic were added to the second stage roster the next day.

With the dates official, I started working on getting tattoo permits for the markets we were playing, and every state was different. Tattooing was still illegal in Massachusetts, so there could be no tattooing of any kind at that show. Several of the states required a brief training for the artists, and inspections of our workspaces (Kansas was the toughest). Others just needed us to file a permit. They all wanted money, and I spent hours every day on the phone, buried under paper, as I navigated arcane state rules and statutes. We invested in equipment to make sure we were compliant and safe: autoclaves, sterilizers, and everything we needed to set up a sterilization tent (which sounds worse than it was). The plan was for each tattoo artist to have their own space, and we bought some sturdy surplus army tents, standing air conditioners for all the tents, chairs, work stations, and lighting.

Our roster of tattoo artists was formidable. Unfortunately, Henk Schiffmacher wasn't one of them. He sent me an email with ideas for how the tour bus should be a hangout and became insulted when I told him his dog, Schatzie, wouldn't be able to come on the road with us. I liked Schatzie, but if anyone was bringing a dog it was going to be me, and I wasn't bringing one. Henk replied with a diatribe about what an insult it was, and how he was the only one who could represent tattooing, and knew tattooing, and on and on. When I showed the email to the other tattoo artists, they decided to vote Henk off the tour. His ego was always going to be a challenge on the road, but I'd wanted him there, and now that wasn't going to happen.

Sean decided that we should have four tattoo artists traveling with us for the tour and arrange to add local artists in markets where there were good ones. Bernie Luther and Filip Leu would be the guest artists on the first half. Filip Leu was arguably the most acclaimed tattoo artist in the world at the time, and getting him was a huge coup (his wife Titine, a painter, traveled with him). Jack Rudy and Gil Monte, both old school tattoo artists from the West Coast, would be the guest artists for the second half of the tour. Sean and Paul Booth, whose macabre black and grey artistry was a favorite of metal bands, would be on the entire tour.

Paul Booth was one of the most popular tattoo artists in the world and had been instrumental in getting Filip Leu to commit to the tour. He had tattooed the members of Slayer, and our bands were already asking about getting appointments with him. He looked like one of Satan's sidekicks: portly, dressed all in black, long black dreads, nose ring, and an attitude that terrified those who didn't know him (he was a big softie underneath). Booth had bought a house in a quiet New Jersey suburb, and his first order of business was to paint it completely black. On the weekends, he would be out spraying pesticide on all the living things on his property so all that was left was dust and dirt. He was authentic, demented, and his tattooing emanated from a wildly creative and eccentric mind; some of his work was disturbing.

Entering Booth's shop in NYC was like entering a dark underworld. As he tattooed the side of my leg below the knee with a monster demon, he and I got a chance to know each other. His style of black and gray tattoo requires a lot of shading, and that requires multiple passes of the machine over already tattooed skin. I never felt such agony. I liked the finished piece, and it nicely complemented my other work. He was a good designer—the interior of his shop was proof of that—and considering the tour's sensibility, we hired him to design the artist tents as well as set decorations for the stage and the festival village.

Stonehenge had always been part of my Tattoo the Earth vision. The first logo I'd made was the words spray painted on a photo of Stonehenge. Booth came up with the idea to build a Stonehenge that people would walk through when they entered the festival village. He showed us drawings of what he was planning, and it was sick, and when I stood in a warehouse in New Jersey staring up at the finished product—an almost full sized, apocalyptic replica of Stonehenge—I was floored and inspired. Until I found out that that each of the three huge sections would have to be cut in half to fit in a truck, and that we would need at least two extra trucks and a crew to take it on tour. On top of that, claiming artistic integrity, Booth hadn't used any flame retardant on the outside layer and Stonehenge wouldn't pass the fire code. In fact, the chemicals he used to make it look amazing made it so super flammable that just sitting in the sun all day could make it immolate. We had to ditch it altogether. It's probably still sitting in that warehouse in Jersey.

Betsy and I were sad and reflective as we prepared to leave for the first show, which was scheduled for Portland, Oregon. Her mother Marsha had died a few months before the tour started, at just 50 years old, and we still felt broken by it. Betsy had been deeply involved in her mother's care, and traveling with the tour promised a welcome change and diversion from what had been a terrible time. Plus, I needed her there with me to watch my back, and keep me sane. Despite everything, including my travails and misadventures, the two of us were doing well. Before we left, she cut her hair short and dyed it blonde, and she looked incredible. We had done this thing together, and we were completely united.

At the airport, I asked how much it would cost to upgrade us to first class. It was over $2,000, just about the amount of credit we had left on our Amex card. We looked at each other, and I knew her answer without having to ask.

"We'll take the upgrade," I said and pulled her closer to me.

Chapter Six

Puya, We Hardly Knew Ya

Sometimes when I would pitch the idea for Tattoo the Earth, I would tell people that my vision of it was so real that I could close my eyes, stand in it, and describe it in detail. I could see it clearly, right from the first moment I had the idea: all the sights, sounds, and smells of it all the way down to my bones. Now I was actually standing smack in the middle of our inaugural show, and while it looked, sounded, and smelled like I'd imagined, it felt nothing like I thought it would. However it went—and there were no guarantees we would get through it in one piece financially or physically—I did feel a sublime sense of accomplishment. I had gone from being one of a million bullshitters hustling some fantastical idea to someone who had seen it through and made it happen. Sixteen thousand people bought a ticket to see our first show. I was looking at them; they were bumping up against me as I wandered about. Under a blistering sunny sky in the middle of a horse track in Oregon, I was standing in the middle of Tattoo the Earth.

But other than this sense of accomplishment, a feeling that I knew from experience was fleeting, I felt nothing but exhaustion and resentment. We were dinged and edgy, hemorrhaging money, with the future of the thing we'd built in constant doubt. Everything had been a struggle, and it never felt like we were ever actually "there." Even then, at our first date, I was still expecting something catastrophic to derail us. I tried to clear my mind of what had been lost getting there and all the minefields we still had to navigate. Nevertheless, I tried to enjoy the moment. Everywhere I turned, though, there were constant reminders of how fucked up everything had gotten, starting with the main stage.

Booth had taken the logo that I'd drawn in my basement—and that was still a trip to see adorning all the swag—and designed a gothic, heavy metal version with red swatches and sharp edges to hang over the stage. I'd approved the designs when he showed them to me, and I thought it was cool that we'd have this imposing logo dominate the stage. But Booth got the measurements wrong, and what was supposed to tower over the stage actually looked like a postage stamp at the top of a legal-sized envelope; you could barely see it from the back of the field. Booth also messed up the two giant scrims with Maori heads that covered the speaker side-fills. The design, which, again, made sense on paper, was actually fine gray print on a black background, and you could barely see it. There were a few times during the day, when the sun hit it just right, that you could sort of see it, but mostly it looked like two black scrims with illegible, faint gray sketching on them. I forgave Booth, for all of it. I'd made plenty of mistakes that had cost us in the lead up, but that was the price of creating something new. You had to be willing to risk big and screw up, and accept the mistake in order to keep the thing moving. I let it all go, as best I could. But Booth couldn't get over it, and he couldn't stop beating himself up, and that was pissing me off.

One thing Booth had gotten right were the tents for the festival village. He'd taken the twenty army tents we bought, done his magic, and made them look like they'd survived the apocalypse (and this time he also managed to incorporate the flame retardant). In addition to the tattoo artists who were traveling with us, the tent village was inhabited by local guest tattoo artists, piercers, henna artists, body painters, record companies and sponsors, and assorted clothing and swag vendors. It looked great when it was all set up, and it was a magic moment when I wound my way through the tents, saw all the kids milling around, and heard the sound of the tattoo machines buzzing. The village, actually the whole set up in Portland, was ideal. Down the field from the main stage was a smaller second stage, and the village sat between them. Our tour manager, Ronnie Hausfeld, aka Mr. Sunshine, was drowning just handling the music piece of the show, and since my role on the tour was undefined (I planned to introduce some bands, do interviews, and play good or bad cop when needed), I volunteered to manage the vendors on the road. Before the tour, we arranged for a group of vendors to travel with us, but some others showed up unexpectedly and joined us for the duration. With all the deals we'd struck with various vendors, and new vendors showing up at each show, it was a real trick collecting the money every night.

"You've got some carny in you, Scott," Zukoski said that first night when I showed him the wad of cash I'd collected. The village was one of the few things that was working, though not without complications.

I'd hired a body painter out of Pahrump, Nevada, named Precious Slut. Slut ran a tattoo and body painting shop, and had done body painting on previous tours; he had a strong portfolio and references. I met Slut for the first time before we opened the doors, and he seemed competent and enthusiastic. His tent looked professional, and he was busy as soon as we let people onto the grounds. But as the venue was filling up, I got a call over the radio to come to Slut's tent. There was a huge crowd in front as well as a couple of cops. The cop in charge told me to go in the tent, and that we would talk after I saw what was happening in there. In the tent, I found six women, most of them underage, in various stages of undress, getting their bodies painted. I think I laughed at first, and then felt like I was going to pass out. Slut was nowhere to be found, so I went over to the cops to gauge the depth of the shit we were in. Seems that Slut had auctioned the painting of the young women to the highest bidder, and after Slut painted them, he would parade them on the table topless or naked while guys crowded around to give them tips. Slut had, in other words, created a little strip club, and the Portland police were having none of it. The age of the girls didn't seem to bother the cops, but the stripping, and guys making contact with the girls, had to cease. They said they'd stop the whole thing but didn't want to start a riot.

"Are you doing this just tonight or are you going on tour with this?" one of the cops asked after I thanked them for being so cool. I told them the cities we were playing, and they chuckled and shook their heads as they wished me luck.

Zukoski thought it was hilarious. We were both open-eyed about how unruly the tour was likely to get, but for this first night we put that behind us and tried to stay focused on just getting through Portland. He also had some good practical advice, like that he and I should try to always be at different ends of the field. That way, if I didn't want to deal with someone I could tell them they'd have to see Zukoski, and he could refer someone he didn't want to deal with to me, and that way we could ping pong people all night. He told me never to carry a radio, so I ditched mine immediately after the Slut incident. Zukoski also said that we finally had the upper hand with the bands now that we were on the road, and that proved true at that first show. We'd been at the mercy of agents and managers, but now it was a new ballgame. Steve Richards showed up, and it was heartbreaking to see him in a wheel chair suffering from what seemed like stroke symptoms; but he was still Steve inside. The band surrounded him, and their affection for him was palpable. I hugged and kissed him, and Clown, and thanked them for sticking with us.

The main stage bands were Slipknot, Slayer, Sepultura,

Sevendust, and hedPe, with Stone Temple Pilots as the headliner for that first show only. The Portland show was presented by the local rock station, and they had booked Stone Temple Pilots to headline their festival, and bought our show to go with it which saved them having to book all the bands themselves. We'd booked a dozen bands for the second stage to travel with us, all up and coming new bands like Cold, Hatebreed, Downset, Full Devil Jacket, and Systematic, and it would prove to be a constant challenge to get every band on and off before curfew. Sometimes the bands on the main and second stage would overlap, and though it sucked, it was usually unavoidable because everyone had to play. We were paying top dollar for the main stage bands, but almost all of the bands on the second stage had their slots paid for by their record company, so the second stage was key for us financially. We'd booked Nashville Pussy to headline the second stage; they were the only band we were paying, and they were the only band giving us grief about the scheduling. That first night, there was no way to schedule their set without it overlapping with Slayer's, and their manager was telling us they wouldn't play if we didn't fix it. We told him to deal with it for the night, and that we'd fix it on the remaining dates, but it quickly became contentious, and I could see Zukoski starting to lose patience.

"I think what we have devolved into here is a circular discussion," the manager said to us condescendingly, like a haughty professor. "And I see no way to resolve this for my band."

"Listen, I don't know about circular discussions," Zukoski began measuredly, though I could see him steaming. "But I have a direction we can go in, and that direction is right out the door. Your band is fired! No circles. No discussions. You're done. Go tell your band."

The manager was stunned as Zukoski and I walked away, and, really, he deserved it. We didn't need to take that shit anymore, at least from the only second stage band we were actually paying. In Zukoski's mind, he'd just saved us money, and made the second stage easier to schedule. The manager tried to smooth it over, but we told him to piss off. Finally, Nashville Pussy's guitarist, Ruyter Suys, came to talk to me. I'd met Ruyter briefly in Europe the previous year when I was traveling with Cypress Hill, and hers was one of the bands I wanted; I thought it was kismet when they were offered to us for the tour. Ruyter was in her early thirties, one of the leading female guitarists in rock, and along with her bass player, Tracy Almazan, one of only two female musicians on the tour. Nashville Pussy were a sleazy hard rock band founded by Ruyter and her husband, Blaine Cartwright, and their insane 1998 debut album, "Let Them Eat Pussy" was nominated for a Grammy. Her stage persona was all about sex, drugs, and wild antics, but sitting across from her backstage I could see that she was prettier than she looked on stage, and more vulnerable.

After I vented and suggested that their manager needed a blanket party (a blanket put over his head while he's pummeled with a mic stand), Ruyter explained that she'd just fired him. She was upset, and said that they hadn't even known he was going to show up that night, and had no idea he was causing such a problem. We groused about managers, agents, and record labels for a while. She told me that Nashville Pussy had almost signed to Sharon Osbourne's record label, and when they met and she told Sharon that Nashville Pussy was doing our tour, Sharon said that she was going to hire a plane to fly over our shows pulling a banner saying "Fuck Tattoo the Earth." I liked Ruyter, and her band, and we decided to let them stay.

I introduced the bands on the main stage in Portland, and I did some emceeing on both stages for the remainder of the tour. I got some advice before I did it for the first time: Scream, curse, and reference the upcoming bands as much as possible.

"How are you motherfuckers doing?" I would scream at the fans. "Are you getting ready for Sepultura? Are you ready for Slayer? Are you ready for Slipknot? Well, you better fucking be ready! Now put your hands together for Sevendust!"

The band that opened the main stage was Famous, Lauren's Bouquette's new band. As our head of guerrilla marketing, Lauren had been instrumental in getting the tour launched, and part of his payoff was having the opening slot on the main stage. Kirby was livid that I'd given the slot to an unknown band without a record deal, but Lauren earned it. I was emotional when I stood in front of the crowd and introduced Famous and then thanked Lauren. The good feeling was lessened slightly when I realized Lauren's band kind of sucked, but he'd earned the spot, and his band was the least of my problems. We still weren't a hundred percent sure what bands were going to show up for that first show, and we still hadn't finalized the last dates of the tour. Coal Chamber had dropped off a week before we started, using the excuse that they needed to get into the studio, and that was a problem. They had been a key band in our package, and a good draw, and we'd have to refund money to the promoters in each place we played because of them. Spineshank showed up unexpectedly to play the second stage, and they were with us for some of the shows. We thought Puya, a progressive metal band from Puerto Rico with a breakthrough album, was going to show up in Portland to play the main stage, but they didn't.

"Puya, we hardly knew ya," Zukoski said when he found out they were a no show.

Someone who did show up in Portland was our tour photographer Fran Strine. In the lead up to the tour, Fran had been trying to get in touch with me by email to see if we needed a photographer, but I hadn't responded. I was buried, mainly answering fans who were ticked off that the dates hadn't been announced yet, and then were angry for all the markets we were missing when dates were announced. Some lambasted us for being another big corporate behemoth who could care less about the fans, when it was just me on my computer at three in the morning in my underwear, getting stoned, answering emails, and dancing for my life. I finally gave Fran my address, and he sent me a nice leather portfolio with his work. His photography looked fine to me, but I was more impressed that the guy had spent so much on a portfolio he knew he probably wouldn't get back. I gave him a call, and listened to his pitch.

"I need to be on this tour," he told me, with a southern drawl. "And I know you don't know me, but I'm tight with the guys from Sevendust, and I've done tons of live shoots, but never a tour, and as soon as I heard about this Tattoo the Earth, I knew I had to be on it. You don't have to pay me, all I need is a spot on a bus. You don't even have to feed me."

In other times, I would have taken pause at Fran's direct approach mixed with desperation, but this was Tattoo the Earth, and the dude was telling me he needed to be there, and that this was his dream. And I did need a photographer, and he'd sent a leather book.

"Listen, Fran" I told him. "If you can get to Portland by July 18, I will put you on a bus, feed you, and give you access to everything. That is assuming you can get to Portland by Saturday, and we don't find out you're an asshole when you get here."

Fran left his job working for a company that made frozen ice cream machines and bought a one-way Greyhound bus ticket from Atlanta to Portland. It took four days, and he got to Portland just in time to join us. I had a good feeling about him immediately, put him on a crew bus, and gave him an all-access backstage pass, the Holy Grail of concert passes.

I tried to listen to as many of the bands as possible that first night, but most of it wasn't my thing. The reality was that I probably wouldn't have attended my own show had someone else put it on. I grew up on the Beatles, the Stones, and the Who, and much of the music on the tour wasn't based in melody. My ears weren't musically wired to get Slayer. But I could appreciate the power and defiance of it, the rock-and-roll middle finger of it. I may have needed a melody to connect to the music, but I got the dark metal sensibility, and knew that if I were sixteen I'd be in the mosh pit banging my head. I felt a connection with the kids at our shows, and they responded when I emceed. I was the head counselor at the most fucked-up summer camp ever.

Sean and I couldn't stop asking each other, "Can you believe this?" I mean, we couldn't believe it.

"You did this bro," he told me, "I never had any doubt."

"We did this, Sean, and I was wracked with doubts."

Sean had been so instrumental in making it happen, and always put the show first. He'd brought in Paul Booth, which took some balls. Booth was an artist of greater stature than he, and most guys would have surrounded themselves with lower-tier guys to protect themselves but not Sean. Sean and Betsy had grown close, and it felt like everything was jibing, and that I was creating a foundation to do big things. I became overcome with emotion thinking about the people who'd helped us get there, like Naomi Fabricant, who quit Jack Utsick and came on the tour as our press liaison and tour manager for the tattoo artists. She was in New Jersey doing the advance work for Giants Stadium, but I called a few times to ask, "Can you believe this?"

"I never doubted it," she replied.

The crowd was going insane by the time Slipknot got ready to take the stage. I could see them as they left their trailer and headed toward me, toward the stage, the future coming closer into focus. I high-fived Clown, and followed the band up to the stage. For an intro, Slipknot had a giant scrim with a pentacle designed that hung in front blocking the stage while the country song, "Get Behind Me Satan" played:

"Get behind me Satan, get behind me Satan,
Get behind me Satan and push.
I'm real darn mad and that's just too bad
Come on Satan and push."

The song distorted as it went on until it was replaced with rapid drumming and total distortion. It built to a climax until the scrim fell, the crowd exploded, and there was fucking Slipknot. The crowd was on the dirt infield, so there was a dust haze over everything, mixed with smoke. During one song, Corey Taylor, Slipknot's front man, got the entire crowd to kneel down with instructions to jump as high as they could when he gave the cue. When the crowd finally jumped up, it was like an implosion, punctuated by a giant mushroom cloud of dirt from the racetrack. It almost knocked me over, the power of it, and my part in making it happen. I thought of Robert Oppenheimer, and how those guys in Los Alamos probably felt the same way. I got chills and started shaking. I fell to my knees and started sobbing uncontrollably. I stayed on my knees and sobbed, until I felt a hand on my shoulder, and looked up to see Zukoski next to me.

"Enjoy this, Scott," he said, his hand squeezing my shoulder. "It'll never feel this way again."

Chapter Seven

The Jockey Shower

Of all the stress-inducing events that made Portland so chaotic, the most traumatic experience was having to take a shower in the jockey locker room after the show. Like the unprepared kid at camp, I had forgotten shower shoes, soap dish, and just about everything I would need on the road. Horse racing wasn't in season, and it looked like everyone had literally abandoned the place after the last race. Betsy kept lookout while I showered, the nozzle, at its highest angle, pointed directly at my chest. I used a dozen towels to lay on the ground, and hopscotched around like in an action movie trying not to make contact with the floor (Fran had to shower in one of the horse stalls, side-stepping manure, which put my own traumatic experience into perspective). I was in denial about traveling on the tour bus but got over it pretty quick on the thirty-hour trip to Lawrence, Kansas. Our bus had Betsy and me, Sean, Booth, the guest tattoo artists, and Naomi Fabricant. The bus consisted of a front part with a lounge, TV, and table, and toward the back were eight coffin-like berths. There was no way I was sleeping in one of the berths. I was collecting money, having meetings, and needed a door that locked. Betsy and I took the back lounge, which had banquettes that we could use for a bed. We learned a hard lesson that first trip from Oregon to Kansas: Not only could you never poop on the bus, but if you needed to make an unscheduled stop for the bathroom, it could cost two or more hours by the time you get back on and off the highway, especially when you're in the middle of nowhere. All the buses, the entire caravan, had to pull over too, because a bus on its own could break down and get stranded. A call would go out over the CBs to the other buses saying there was an unscheduled stop, and then everyone would get out, and invariably someone would go missing. Betsy had to go on that first trip, and fortunately so did one of the henna artists who'd had an unfortunate reaction to a corn dog, so that gave her cover, but she still had a terrible walk of shame. (I don't think Betsy went to the bathroom for the rest of the tour.) Neither of us slept at all that first night. I felt wired and my head was ringing, like I was coming down from an acid trip. I don't know if I had ever been so tired or worried, or so satisfied. The next morning, when I looked in the mirror, I noticed a dime-sized white patch in my stubble; Tattoo the Earth, and the jockey shower, had turned me gray overnight.

It felt like we'd been on the bus for a month by the time we hit Kansas, and we still weren't sure who was going to be on the bill, though we figured if someone was willing to make that long trip, they were in it for the long-haul. The venue in Lawrence was a small community park, and unlike the racetrack in Portland, which at least had some sort of infrastructure, everything in Burcham Park had to be built from scratch, in a space barely big enough to fit both stages, which made things more cacophonous when both of them were in action at the same time. There was a huge branch hanging over the top of the stage, and a four-foot spigot right in front of the stage, and we recommended that they bring in a plumber to cut the spigot off at ground level because it would take a hot minute for the fans to break it off. They didn't, the fans snapped it during the first set, and the pristine grass soon became a mud pit. Fans were pelting the stage with clumps of sod, covering all the band equipment with it, and forcing the musicians to be on their toes or get hit. Tom Araya, Slayer's front man, got hit right in the face with a piece of sod, stopped playing, and wouldn't start again until it stopped. Slipknot had that large scrim that hung in front of the stage, and fans in the pit bombarded the scrim before the band started, and then it was like a wall of mud heaved at the band when the scrim dropped. Later on, they washed the scrim, but let it dry in the sun, and it shrunk and never fell correctly for the rest of the tour.

Slipknot had hired pyro technicians to design and run pyrotechnics for their show, though they couldn't do it in Portland because they didn't get permits in time. The team doing it had experience in the movie industry, but this was their first concert tour. I was standing by the back of the field when they did the first round of fire cannons, and it looked out of proportion for the size of the stage. There was only supposed to be one flash, and the band started to move forward after the first one, then a second one boomed, spitting out fire from the side of the stage for an even longer duration. When the pyro finally stopped, I could see that the stage side fills were smoldering, but fortunately the huge branch hadn't gone up in flames. The crew had broken out the fire extinguishers, and as I rushed to the stage I heard Corey Taylor talking to the crowd.

"You never know if you're going to live or die at one of our shows," he told them.

Once on the stage, I got into a shouting match with the pyro tech, at one point screaming so loud that we distracted the band while they played. Offstage, the guy told me this was part of first night adjustments, and that's why the duration was so long. I told him no more pyro until we saw a plan, and the band backed it up. Clown and Danny Nozell, Slipknot's tour manager, were apologetic, and angry themselves—Clown came close to being seriously burned up there.

Danny was one of the sane voices during the tour, a solid rock amid the turmoil. Zukoski and I met with Clown and Danny on the tour bus, along with Paul Grey, the bassist, and Joey Jordison, the drummer. Clown, Paul, and Joey had founded Slipknot in Des Moines in 1995, and represented the band. Offstage they were soft-spoken, and grateful for the opportunity, and we expressed a similar sentiment. They were never anything but professional and reasonable. On stage, once the jumpsuits and masks went on, it was fucking chaos. Danny was the perfect tour manager for them. When I was a kid, I'd worked a show for the British punk band The Damned that turned into a riot, and their tour manager was the nicest guy ever, in tan slacks and light blue sweater, like your guide for a weekend at an estate. Danny had that same vibe. He never lost his composure, and could work out any problem. Without someone like Danny, the tour would have devolved into an even lower level of hell.

After our show, Burcham Park looked like a post-nuclear scene out of *Terminator 2*. The entire field was destroyed, and the stage was charred, smoldering, and completely caked with mud.

"We left our mark here, bro," Sean said as we looked at the damage.

I laughed but knew how close we had come to disaster. My greatest fear was that someone would die at one of our shows because of something stupid that we did; I had recurring nightmares about it in the weeks leading up to the tour. Zukoski's recurring nightmare was that no customers showed up. His wife would sometimes find him sleep-walking, looking out the bedroom window and asking where all the people were. The pyro mishap shook me, and I began to doubt that we could make it through the tour without a major calamity. I checked with the EMS workers to see if anyone got hurt, but there was nothing major. Metal shows usually didn't have serious injuries; the fans are big, and experienced moshers, and it's like a sport for them. Punk and pop shows were the worst, the EMTs told me, because the fans are young, and many times it's their first concert, and they jump into the pit and get the shit kicked out of them.

We had to leave Kansas right away to get the rest of the way across the country to Giants Stadium, to a show that was the biggest landmine of all. I kept getting asked if I was excited about the show, and the answer was I had the same excitement as before an invasive medical procedure. We set up our main stage in the parking lot, and the second stage bands would play out there. When the bands on that stage finished, the main stage bands would start inside the stadium, with Metallica closing the show. At one point, about three in the morning the night before the show, Betsy and I were standing on the stage, and we were the only ones in the entire stadium.

"Can you believe we did this thing?" I said, putting my arms around her. Clown and Naomi soon joined us there, and we all took it in for a while. The general consensus was, how the fuck did this happen? It was the sublime moment of the tour for me, and I should have gone home right after because it all went to shit from there.

There was no tattooing at the show, even though tattooing was legal in New Jersey, and we didn't even set up the festival village. We were told that there would be no way to secure the tents on the concrete, so we couldn't set up in the parking lot (though we saw giant slabs and barrels for that exact purpose all around the facility). We put some of our tents in the spiral staircase abutting the stadium, but when that didn't work, we shelved the whole village. At lunch, I was approached by two union guys who told me I had to sign a release, and pay a fee to do any filming, even for archival footage. They had seen Fran filming some early second stage bands on his Camcorder, and said I needed to pay them $1,000 to be able to use it. I told them that no one on my crew would do any filming, and I'd have Fran delete the footage he took. But they wouldn't let it go, and followed me when I walked away, literally fast-walk chasing me down the concourse trying to get me to cough up a grand.

"Yeah, they can stick to you like that," Zukoski said when I told him the story about the union guys.

It was Zukoski's birthday, and we took some time alone to plan and reflect.

"On this day," he said, "you and me, we put on the biggest show in the world. We'll always have this, Scott."

From there, I went on stage to introduce a band, passing many of the agents, managers, promoters, and record execs who'd put up roadblocks, and who continued to hurt our chances for success.

"I want to thank all of you motherfuckers for coming today and making Tattoo the Earth possible. You made this happen," I told the crowd. "And to those who tried to stop us, many of whom are here today, I want to tell you, sincerely, to go fuck yourselves."

Everybody couldn't help but stick their claws in Tattoo the Earth, and they sucked as much from us as they could. When we did the financial settlement after the show, John Scher, the promoter, told us that five hundred Coal Chamber fans came to the box office asking for refunds because the band had canceled, and he was deducting it from our take. We were never going to make a lot of money on the Giants Stadium show, and didn't care because of the prestige it afforded us, but now we weren't making anything, and there was nothing we could do about it. They charged me for parking, so I was actually twenty-five dollars in the hole for the honor of playing there.

We did the financial settlement in the bowels of the stadium in a room that looked like a bank with teller windows, and as Zukoski and I were walking back to the stage, we saw and heard some bikers coming toward the back gate. These gates are typically impenetrable, but the bikers didn't even have to slow down as the gates opened for them. They were there for Booth, something about him not having given them a heads up about the show and being disrespectful. Booth is a huge guy, but one of the bikers had him off the ground against a wall backstage, poking him in the chest. Zukoski and I just walked by. This was Booth's business, and it shook him pretty bad.

Unlike in Germany, Metallica did not allow me or anyone on the tour to watch them. Once Slipknot finished their set, they cleared the stage and no one was allowed on when Metallica played. I could hear them playing while I hung out near the buses and got drunk with some of the bands. It seemed a fitting way for the show to end. But we got what we wanted from the show, and it was a dream come true for many of our bands, so I considered it successful.

The next stop was an amphitheatre in Scranton, and that was a breeze compared to the first three shows because we didn't have to build it from scratch. On the road it hit me what we'd lost when Clear Channel pulled their shows. Not only were we missing major markets (including the entire Southeast), but we were struggling in some of the markets we had left. Ticket sales were weak, and we were struggling with the challenges presented by alternate venues. Venues like Suffolk Downs horse race track, known in racing circles as "suffering downs," was used as the location for our show in Boston. It was my hometown show, and I was actually looking forward to it. Mark Sokol, the local production manager, was an early advocate for the project. He worked for the promoter, Mass Concerts, and I'd first met him at a show at the Palladium in Worcester. He'd been sitting at a table outside the venue checking in the bands for a festival, and I gave him a promo card, and we started talking. He loved the idea, and had some good advice, and had pumped up Tattoo the Earth to his boss at Mass Concerts. Now they were presenting our show in Boston.

I was excited to see Mark when I crawled out of the bus for breakfast, but he had already gotten into a fight with our tour manager, Ronnie, over the catering, and both of them were bent out of shape. It was the usual bullshit between touring veterans who get off on the wrong foot, but fuck, man. Anytime I'd imagine an aspect of the tour beforehand, the reality invariably ended up being the exact opposite. I envisioned Ronnie and Mark as buddies, and hanging out, and now they only talked to each other through intermediaries. The thing that set them off was that breakfast was late, and nothing pisses off a crew like late meals. Typically, the promoter takes care of the catering, but Zukoski had seen an opportunity to make some extra money and told the promoters to give us whatever they were going to pay a caterer and that we would handle it. We were five shows into the tour, and that decision was already haunting us. Outback Jack, the caterer he hired, had done the Warped Tour, but Jack had failed to mention that he'd also gotten thrown off it. Catering had been provided in Portland, so Kansas was the first show Outback Jack would cater, and they were late, claiming that a vehicle had broken down. They blew breakfast, and then barely had it together for lunch and dinner. We cut Outback Jack some slack because they had travel issues, but the food for the next show was mediocre, and consisted of hamburgers, hot dogs, beans, and buns (Naomi, who was vegan, was reduced to eating bean sandwiches). The Jack of Outback Jack was haggard, and apologetic, but that didn't assuage the bands and crew who were rightfully angry about it (I was out there eating the same crap and felt the same way).

So it was not surprising that catering had caused the kerfuffle between Ronnie and Mark. No one knew why breakfast was half set-up (there was no coffee, which was causing a full-on panic), and two of the women who worked catering were missing. The mystery was solved when Naomi went to take a shower, and the door was locked. She banged on the door, and when it finally opened, she saw that the two caterers were having sex in the shower room. Naomi told them the crew was freaking out, and to get back to work.

"We'll get around to it," one of them told Naomi, and closed the door. I was losing patience with Outback Jack.

As had been the case in Portland, our show was a local hard rock radio station's annual concert event—Boston's WAAF—and, barring weather or catastrophe, was almost a guaranteed success since the station had promoted the living shit out of it. It was a beautiful day, and the setup of the stages and village were the best they'd been. It was just how I always envisioned Tattoo the Earth— except that we couldn't tattoo. The same hepatitis scare that had once inspired the ban on tattooing in New York had done the same in Massachusetts, and though it looked like the law was starting to crack, the only tattooing allowed was with henna. I'd been up front with the tattoo artists from the beginning that things were going to be fucked up at times and had told them when those times were most likely to occur. Sean was with the program—he knew what was going on behind the scenes—as was Bernie. But Booth was uptight. He was already on edge because his set designs hadn't worked out, and his run-in with the bikers at Giants Stadium had only made things worse. Booth felt that tattooing was like a side note for us, and that the art form, and the artists, weren't being treated with respect, but he was alone in feeling that way. For the other artists, if they had to sit out in New Jersey and Boston for reasons beyond our control, then that was cool, just part of the journey. We were all in uncharted territory, and felt like explorers, especially Filip Leu, who was completely open to the experience.

Filip had grown up traveling the world with his parents, Felix and Loretta, both tattooists and painters, and his three siblings; they were a nomadic tattooing hippie family. Filip began tattooing professionally when he was ten, and did his own traveling to study with the great tattoo masters in Asia, Europe, and the US. Maybe he was travelled out, given that now he rarely left Switzerland, where his shop was located. The family had settled in Lausanne in the eighties, and named their studio The Leu Family's Family Iron. Filip had long black hair that he sometimes put up into a kind of bun, kept in place with what looked like big ivory knitting needles. He had fine, exotic features, and was razor thin. He had a tribal tattoo that went up his Adam's apple to the base of his chin, and wore a necklace made from the teeth his father had lost after a bout of mouth cancer. His father was still ailing, which was one of the reasons Filip was only doing half the tour. Filip and Titine added a calm to the storm we were in.

Since Filip couldn't tattoo at the Boston show, he tattooed me a little, jumping in on Bernie's sleeve. He and Bernie were friends, and he knew Bernie would first get angry when he saw that his work had been fucked with, and then grudgingly accept it when he learned that Filip was the culprit. That night, Filip fixed a tattoo that Betsy had on her shoulder. She had gotten her first tattoo when we first met, and before I knew what was what with tattooing. She wanted a variation on a sun she saw on the cover of a King Crimson album, but it turned out badly, and was indecipherable. Sean tried to fix it, but Betsy didn't want to make it any larger, and he could only do so much. Filip convinced her to make it bigger, and the finished result was a mind blower, a sort of sun, sunflower design. She finally loved it, and we were just in awe of his talent.

Despite the distractions, Boston was a strong show for us, but not for the Revere neighborhood surrounding the racetrack. The day after our show, the mayor called an emergency meeting and effectively banned Tattoo the Earth and Slipknot for life. Turns out that we were so loud, and the banter and cursing between songs so raunchy, that citizens on the outskirts of Revere were driving around looking for the source of the party so they could shut it down. Those closest to the track took to the phones and showed up at the box office. We'd also trashed the shrubbery and flowers in the center of the infield, among other sundry infractions. There had only been a handful of concerts at Suffolk Downs prior to ours: The Beatles in 1966, The Jackson 5 in 1973, and, just a few days before us, in the first concerts in twenty-seven years: the Guinness Fleadh Festival, and Warped Tour. All was okay, until Slipknot and the rest of Tattoo the Earth were permanently exiled from what would end up being one of our best venues.

The next show in Cleveland was the last straw for Outback Jack. They could just not get it together. Zukoski was back in New Jersey, so it was up to me to fire Jack and his wife. After listening to our overwhelming list of grievances, they had no choice but to walk off hand in hand into the dark. Catering would be hit or miss for the rest of the tour, mostly miss. In addition to being a massive pain in the ass, it was terrible for morale, hurt us financially, and the anxious uncertainty about whether we'd be fed and whether the food would be edible hung over every show. In the meantime, I bought a few barbecue grills, and ordered pizzas every night to keep Slayer happy.

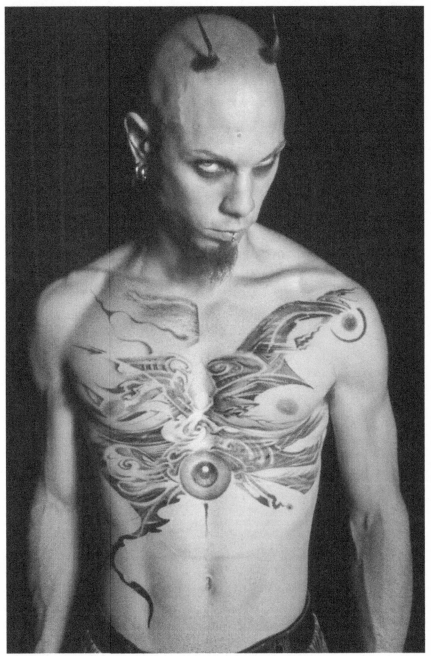

Ryan Martinie (Mudvayne)

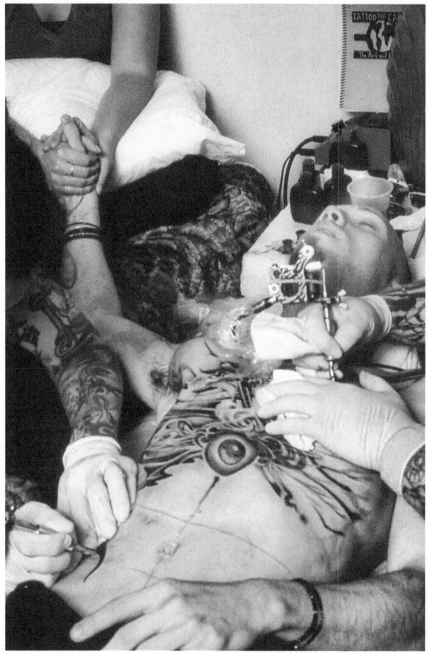

Ryan Martinie being tattooed by Filip Leu and Paul Booth

Tom Araya (Slayer)

Paul Gray (Slipknot)

Jared Gomes (Hed PE)

John Connolly (Sevendust)

Josh Brown (Full Devil Jacket)

Sid Wilson (Slipknot) with Filip Leu

Casey Chaos (Amen)

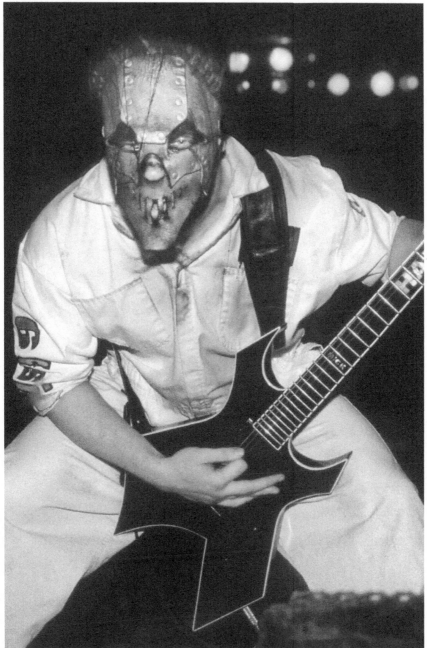

Mick Thomson (Slipknot)

Scott Weiland (Stone Temple Pilots)

Paul Booth demonstrates tattoo aftercare on Andreas Kisser (Sepultura)

Sonny Mayo (Amen)

Scooter Ward (Cold)

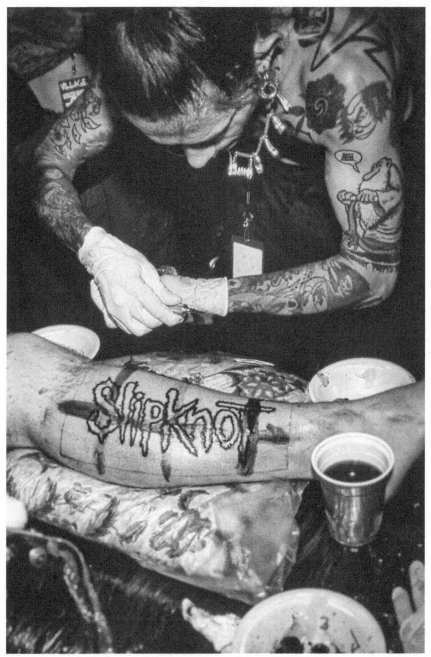

Shawn Crahan gets a collaborative tattoo

Chapter Eight

Wisconsin Death Trip

Of all the venues on the tour, the World Golf Dome in Bridgeview took the dubious prize as the most alternative. We put a summer festival in an indoor golf driving range, and everything about it just sucked. The venue was a pressurized dome, so load-in took forever because we needed to pause in a narrow hallway with each load of equipment, repressurize, and then head through the next door. We made triple sure that the pyro guys didn't set up because I could see them blowing the dome right off the place. The venue was surreal once people were inside, and the bands started playing on both stages; it was a steaming hot, cacophonous mess. I had a thought to go up to the second level and hit golf balls into the crowd, but it seemed like too much effort. One bright spot was the caterer we hired for the show, who put out an appealing selection of barbecue. Everyone was excited to pile up a plate with ribs, chicken, and actual vegetables. Until a crew member bit into a huge piece of glass, and started bleeding from his mouth. Everyone stared dejectedly at the food piled on their plates, and then threw it all in the garbage.

Tattooing was illegal in Bridgeview, but the mayor gave us a special permit to do some demonstrations. The mayor failed to inform the local police of that fact, though, and they started harassing us right when the doors opened. Then word came down that there was something wrong with Filip's visa (there wasn't), and the local police were coming to take him in. Naomi ran to his tent, and told him that they had to go, right then, and right away. Filip started grabbing his equipment, but Naomi said she would take care of it, and that they needed to leave immediately. Naomi and Filip fought their way through the venue, but it was so crowded they could barely move; there were people throwing up and passed out from the heat. They ran out the back of the building and had to wait to get pressurized before they could leave (they were convinced the police would trap them in there). Once they got out, they ran over some dirt mounds, stumbling down until they were in the bus and safely hidden away. The cops stopped all the tattoo demonstrations, for no other reason than that they could, and it pissed us off.

I did interviews with the *Chicago Tribune* and a local TV station, ranting about how we were being harassed, and how our freak show could not be stopped. Booth didn't like that I was giving the interviews, and didn't think I should be representing tattooing. I told him I was representing Tattoo the Earth, not speaking for tattooing, and that he could talk to them the next time if he wanted. I wanted whatever was best for the tour. I was emceeing because it needed to be done, and didn't particularly want to do it; I found it to be a pain in the ass. But people seemed to be responding, I was getting better at it, and the bands appreciated the intro.

"We've got Sean Vasquez, Paul Booth, Filip Leu, and Bernie Luther, some of the best tattoo artists in the world," I would say to the crowd. "Someone's gonna bleed today."

Then I'd point to someone in the front. "It might be you, motherfucker."

Or I'd go off on some riff about tattooing the moon. Doing interviews and introducing bands established me as the face of the brand, and it irked Booth that the face was a tattoo outsider.

Our next stop was Waterworks Park in Des Moines, Slipknot's hometown show. Like Kansas, this was not a suitable stop for us, and we didn't sell a whole lot of tickets. The morning started ominously when one of the crew went into a Porta-Potty during load-in and the Porta-Potty got picked up by a forklift and taken all the way to the other side of the field. He was covered in blue goo when he finally escaped, and we were all terrified to use them after that. We hired a local caterer, and the spread was the worst so far; cold cuts and dressings sitting out in hundred degree heat. Even the flies took a pass. And once the bands started, and the local promoter heard the volume, and non-stop cursing from the stage, the rest of the show was fraught. The local promoter wanted me to do something about the cursing, as if I would, or could. If I told the bands not to say "motherfucker," they'd go right on stage and tell the crowd that "some cocksucking motherfucker told us not to say motherfucker." There weren't a whole lot of love songs played on the tour.

By that time in the tour, I'd gotten to know most of the second stage bands. The main stage bands were more aloof—I don't think I saw Tom Araya from Slayer the entire tour—but the second stage bands were all grateful they'd gotten the support of their record company and a slot on the tour. On the best of days, most of the second stage bands got to play twenty minutes, which meant twenty-three-and-half hours of waiting around to play a couple of songs. On amphitheater shows, where we had to put all the bands on one stage, we'd have to cut some bands, or shorten sets to ten minutes, and have bands play just as the doors opened. Nashville Pussy once played a twelve-minute set and bragged that it was the best per-hour rate the band had ever been paid. The tour was a tough gig, but the new bands had a record out, and this was the best way to promote it before they headed off on their own tours.

I know that Slipknot was bummed that we didn't sell more tickets, but there were a lot of reasons behind it. We'd put our tickets on sale late; the market was saturated with lifestyle tours; it was a non-traditional venue (people tend to go to venues they are familiar with); and our line-up just wasn't strong enough to break though those obstacles. But the disappointment made them emotional, and Slipknot played one of their better shows of the tour. I stood in the crowd and watched them for a while, and it was mesmerizing. The whole thing was a sonic assault, but once I took it in, and let my defenses down, it was exhilarating. Sid, the DJ, was climbing on the scaffolds, and dove into the crowd. All of them played with such reckless abandon (Joey's drumming was the fastest I've ever seen), it was amazing they weren't seriously hurt, and could do that night after night. The dedication to their music and fans was astounding, and the fans responded by losing it at every show.

"It's only about two things," Corey Taylor would tell the crowd. "You and us."

I was getting into their set, and I knew some of that interest could be chalked up to musical Stockholm Syndrome; listen to anything enough times, and you'll eventually start becoming engaged. But I liked Slipknot, and it was a triumphant show for them. Unfortunately, a few weeks after the show, not only did Slipknot and Tattoo the Earth get banned from WaterWorks Park, but all concerts were banned from WaterWorks Park in perpetuity. We'd played eight shows, and been banned for life by two of them.

"I'm getting sick of this," I vented to Sean Vasquez. "They won't let us tattoo, they fucking ban us, they're treating us like shit, and it's not right, man."

"Dude, you can't be serious," Sean said laughing. "You came to Iowa with a bunch of tattoo artists, and fucking Slipknot and Slayer, to tattoo their children, and you're upset you didn't get a parade. How did you think they were going to react?"

"Hey man, I'm just a mixed-up kid from Long Island trying to entertain the kids," I told him. "We come in peace, dude, but fuck 'em if they can't see the future."

"That's all great, bro, but get ready because it's only going to get worse."

The whole enterprise seemed like it was getting darker and more dangerous as we headed west and then south. The vibe was foreboding the moment we set foot at our next stop, Float-Rite Park in Somerset, Wisconsin. Our show was part of the 93X Clambake, the local rock radio station's annual festival, but the mood was anything but festive. During the day at most shows, Clown liked to take a golf cart into the festival village to check out the crowd and listen to some of the bands. He was anonymous without his mask, and enjoyed the freedom of driving around and seeing what he had wrought. In Somerset, Clown took out a golf cart with Fran, Sonny Mayo from Amen, and a few others (golf carts were definitely one of the best parts of the tour). I'd made the right call about Fran. The bands trusted him, and they all gave him complete access onstage and off. Fran said Kerry King from Slayer approached him in Lawrence (Kerry is an intimidating character, and Fran first thought he'd done something to piss Kerry off), but Kerry told him to come up on stage and shoot away. Fran was a talented photographer, reliable, and a good hang.

Clown, Fran, and Sonny were cruising around Float-Rite Park, when out of nowhere, Clown got clotheslined by a security guard, and the cart flipped on its side. Then the security guard maced them at close distance while they were still on the ground. Within seconds they were all rolling on the ground, gasping for breath. Fran said it was the closest he ever felt to dying. They got Clown close up, right in the face, and he was vomiting, snot pouring from his nose. He was having serious trouble breathing, so paramedics put him on oxygen and got him back to his bus. We weren't sure if he would be able to play that night, or whether he should. The head of the venue's security had maced the leader of the headline band a few hours before the show, and we weren't sure if it would be safe for them to play.

"I'm not in this fucking thing to cancel," Zukoski bellowed over the phone when we filled him in on the situation. "We're going to get paid tonight, so work it out."

We met with the promoter, and the security team, and our tour manager Ronnie told me not to engage with the head of security.

"I know you want to rip into that guy, but we need to just keep our mouths shut, play, get paid, and get out of here," Ronnie said seriously. "These motherfuckers are crazy. You don't want to mess with these people." He shook his head. "Wisconsin, man."

The head of security had a strange, smug look when we met to get assurances that the band would not be bothered again. They said Clown was driving recklessly, ignoring instructions, and made obscene gestures, which I knew was bullshit. Who did what didn't matter at this point, and Ronnie tried to keep everyone focused. The promoter asked that the band not mention the incident from the stage. We agreed, and asked that the head of security be nowhere near the band for the rest of the night. So they played—Clown didn't want to cancel, either—but we had our people positioned around the band during their set in case shit broke loose. I saw the head of security lurking around, but decided not to confront him. The show was brutal. It was the only show where event staff pushed the fans back into the moshpit. Typically, they pull them into a space in front of the stage, and let them walk around back into the crowd (or to EMS if they got beat up). But at this event staff were pushing them all back in, and it was causing a weird dynamic, like water crashing against a dam. It was tense, and I wouldn't have any sense of relief until we were all out of there and on the highway.

Precious Slut, my rogue body painter, didn't make it out of Somerset. When word spread about the incident, Slut started ranting about what happened at his body painting tent, and was getting the crowd agitated. And that was it for Slut. He had been a pain in the ass since his impromptu underage strip club in Portland, and every show had been a test of how far he could push the boundaries. The promoter in Cleveland wouldn't even let him set up. Slut also had a number of nefarious and illegal activities going on, and now he was trying to start a riot, so I fired him, and had someone drive him to the airport. I had our entire touring party locked down in their buses until we broke down the equipment and were on our way. I found out later that Clown's macing was retribution for an incident that had occurred when Slipknot played the venue with Ozzfest the previous year. The band had been unhappy with how they were treated, and one of them took a shit on the dressing room floor. The macing was payback; Tattoo the Earth got sandwiched between the shit and the mace.

The next show was at The Eagles Ballroom, a landmark venue in Milwaukee, where we took an outdoor festival and put it into a 3500-seat club. The village was outside in a section of the parking lot covered with jagged pieces of gravel. The tattoo artists had finally had it, and said they weren't going to tattoo. Naomi had developed a good rapport with the artists and got to work trying to calm the situation. When she'd joined the tour in Kansas, Sean Vasquez told her to take one of the top sleeping berths on the bus, that those were the most comfortable. Everyone had a good laugh when Naomi came flying out of the bunk the first time the bus time took a tight turn. She was a good sport, good company, super organized, and the artists knew that she was there to advocate for them.

Surrounded in the Rave Nightclub, Naomi asked them what she could do for them. What could she do to make them happy?

"Get us some paper and drawing pencils, and let us draw," Filip replied.

So Naomi went out and found some large sheets of paper and charcoal pens, carved out some open space on one of the club's floors, and turned four big round tables on their side to make an easel. The four tattoo artists each started at one of the tables, and then after twenty minutes they each shifted to another, and took up where the previous artists had left off. They continued rotating, and the finished pieces were an amalgam of the four artists, and unique.

They drew a crowd, and people were taken in by the process. They dubbed it the Art Fusion Experiment, and it was good to see the artists happy (especially Booth). It had been a tough tour for them, and this was a highlight so far.

As I walked through the crowd to get to the village, I stopped to watch Sevendust. I was able to shut off everything for a song, and get into the music and the crowd. They were one of my favorites on the tour, and were one of the most accessible bands; Sevendust loved to hang. Their rock & roll roots, and their mix of melodic and heavy, appealed to me, and I tried to watch some of their set every night. Standing there in the Eagles Ballroom, smelling the stale beer and reefer, I was lost in the moment, then snapped out of it and went outside to check on the village. As I got near the village, I saw an EMT taking away a young guy whose face was bleeding. I thought there must have been a fight, but it turned out the guy had decided to pierce his face fifteen times in an ill-advised effort to finagle a backstage pass. The police grabbed him when the fourth face piercing, with a four inch needle, drew a crowd, and the blood started flowing. The EMTs cleaned him up, and he was later seen with small Band-Aids all over his face watching Slipknot.

He wasn't the only one injured that night. Fran, fresh off his macing in Somerset, was standing in front of the stage shooting Slayer, with his elbows resting on the stage as he balanced the camera. A huge fan came body-surfing out of the moshpit, and landed on top of him, smashing his eye into the camera and splitting his eyebrow. The EMTs suggested he go to the hospital to get some stitches, but that could take a long time, and we were planning to shove off as soon as the gear was loaded. They put a butterfly stitch on it, and suggested he get the dressing changed by the EMTs in the next city, and that's what he did, in city after city, until it healed. He and I were standing outside the building, and someone told us a car parked right in front of us belonged to Jeffrey Dahmer. Dahmer had killed his first victim a few blocks away at the Ambassador Hotel, and the owner of the car vouched for its authenticity as the last car Dahmer owned.

"Wisconsin," Fran said, shaking his head.

Some artists from Slipknot's local tattoo shop were in Milwaukee, and Clown wanted to get the Slipknot logo tattooed on the side of his calf. Filip, still in the collaborative spirit of the Art Fusion Experiment, talked Clown into getting a collaborative tattoo by all the artists. They set up in a dressing room, and over the course of a few hours, Filip, Booth, Bernie, Sean, and the guys from his home shop tattooed Clown at the same time. Getting tattooed by multiple people is no joke, but Clown toughed it out; this was a guy who could take some pain. We all realized that Fran didn't have any tattoos and talked about hog-tying him at the next show and tattooing him on stage. Clown was deep into his tattoo when he asked me if I wanted to tattoo him, and with Filip over my shoulder, I tattooed someone for the first time. I had a small area to fill in, and my heart was jumping as I got the needle close to his skin. Just as I made contact, Clown fake-screamed, and I nearly leapt out of my shoes.

The next night, in Pontiac, Michigan, it was my turn. Tattooing the public wasn't possible because the village was washed out by rain, so Bernie finished the sleeve he'd started on me in Berlin.

"Who did this?" Bernie screamed, when he looked over my arm and saw what Filip had added to the design.

Some tattoo pieces take multiple sessions to finish, sometimes over a period of years, so the artist likes to carefully look over the work to remind him what he's been creating and to see if the owner has been taking care of the tattoo. Sean used to chastise clients for hanging their arms out car windows, and getting too much sun on his work.

When I told Bernie it was Filip who added to his design, he laughed, and begrudgingly accepted it, just as Filip had predicted.

"At least he didn't ruin it," Bernie muttered.

I don't know if I was tired or what, but I suffered and struggled while Bernie worked on my arm. Granted, he was tattooing my elbow, but I'd been through much worse. Filip said the best painkiller is wanting it, and I guess I didn't want it in Pontiac. I did want the sleeve finished, though, and seeing the final version was a great moment. That day, Filip did a serpent demon chest piece on Lajon Witherspoon from Sevendust, and one of his trademark skulls on the forearm of Sid from Slipknot. Booth tattooed a sun/moon on Corey Taylor's chest; he tattooed Igor Cavalera and Andreas Kisser from Sepultura, and John Connolly from Sevendust. The Tattoo the Earth musicians were awash in skulls, demons, and monsters. Filip and Booth did a collaborative chest piece on Ryan Martinie from Mudvayne, a freehand mix of their dark and tribal styles with an eyeball at its center. Ryan was in agony toward the end of the tattoo, but played his set right after, as did Lajon. Both Ryan and Lajon said that playing live in the wake of a post-tattoo endorphin rush was an almost spiritual experience.

The show in Pontiac took place in the parking lot of the Phoenix Plaza, and though there was a driving rainstorm the entire day, we had a crowd of 10,000 people. It was too rainy to set up for tattooing, and the village was just about washed out. I introduced a few of the bands, standing in an inch of water. The rain was coming in sideways, and sound and light rigs were swaying. I started with my usual bullshit: "Are you motherfuckers ready for Mudvayne?" when a sparkplug went whizzing by my ear and hit a cymbal. The thing was zooming, and would have been deeply imbedded in my skull if it had been thrown a few inches to the right. That was it for emceeing that night. It's weird how people threw things that were native to their local area; a bratwurst got thrown at the stage in Milwaukee; a barbecued turkey leg in Texas.

Not only did the tattooing get washed out, but I needed to refund the vendors because the day was a bust for them. Depending on what challenge we faced, I was cutting deals with vendors at each show, and trying to keep everyone happy, especially those who were out there selling their wares to make a living. A bunch of the vendors were from record companies, or were sponsors, and they were giving things away, not selling, so they didn't care. JNCO sent out a young guy to staff their booth, and the kid traded a tours' worth of promotional items for blow jobs. In just a couple of shows, he got thrown off the tour.

We recorded the show in Pontiac for a live album, and it was a minor miracle that we were able to pull it off. Before the tour, Zukoski had arranged a lucrative deal for a live recording, but Slayer's management put the kibosh on it with their demands and restrictions. We were still hoping to salvage the deal as we started the tour, but Slayer again nixed it, and also demanded additional lights, at considerable cost, even though the majority of their shows took place before it got dark. Pontiac was one of the few shows where we actually used them. Between the lights, the blown record deal, and overpaying them for the shows, Slayer were costing us a chunk of money. We were all pissed when the deal fell through, but Steve Richards's brother Gary stepped in and put together a deal with his record company. We weren't going to make as much, the deal didn't have the same distribution, and we would only have one opportunity to record one show, but it was better than nothing. The undone deal soured an already contentious relationship with Slayer's management. The music business bullshit was a constant hum of obstruction and pettiness, and more irritating and frustrating with each show.

Chapter Nine

Not Since the Donner Party

Trying to find the right spot for the tattoo artist's tents at each show was like NASA trying to figure out where to safely land a space probe on Mars. Ronnie and Naomi walked the venues looking for the perfect spot that would keep the artists in the shade the longest (sunset could be unbearable). Unfortunately, it was over 100 degrees at our first Texas stop at the Far West Rodeo in San Antonio, and no amount of planning could make that okay. We added additional standing air conditioners and fans to the artist tents, but it was unbearably hot with the sun beating down, and dry and dusty; the ground was so baked it had giant cracks in it. Everyone was suffering from the heat; my freshly tattooed arm was roasting in the sun, even with a long sleeve shirt on. Nashville Pussy played at sunset every day, and the sun hit them like lasers, and produced some strange tan lines. It took its toll on Ruyter Suys, their guitarist, who at many shows stripped to her underwear, climbed the scaffolding, and then after the set ran straight to catering and jumped in the giant tub filled with ice and drinks. Ruyter was having a great tour. At one of our shows, she ran into a guy she knew in high school who'd been the hot shot guitarist in town back then. He was a few years older, she'd been a bratty teenage guitar player who followed him around, and he'd wanted nothing to do with her. His band was on Tattoo the Earth for that show only, and played on the second stage before the doors opened. When he asked what she was doing there, and she told him she was headlining the second stage, his mouth dropped, and she enjoyed one of those "you shouldn't have underestimated me, motherfucker" moments.

We played four shows in Texas, none of them sold enough tickets, and all of them were infernos. One independent promoter had bought all the Texas shows. He got creamed in San Antonio, and it didn't look any better for the other shows. Ozzfest and Warped Tour played the day before or after us for some of the shows, and that hurt all of us. After the first show it was going to take a miracle for the rest of the Texas swing to break even, and the whole enterprise was getting tired and sloppy. One of the stage riggers got hurt setting up the lighting, which was a result of lousy routing, alternative venues, and the heat. Fran was shooting Amen, who were like a modern day Sex Pistols, and were unpredictable on stage. I'd loved punk rock in the 1970s, and Amen spoke to those roots. Fran shot them every day because he never knew what crazy shit they were going to do. In San Antonio, Fran was perched on the corner of the stage when the bass player kicked a mic stand, and the heavy bell at the bottom of the stand hit Fran in the head and knocked him out cold; he woke up in an ambulance on the way to the hospital. The members of Slipknot were also getting injured, and they were having their own internal struggles and strife, in addition to a grueling tour, and that night Clown shaved the hair off his stage mask, which made it even creepier.

We hired a caterer in San Antonio for the four Texas shows, dependent on how the catering was for the first show. The caterer pulled out all the stops: chicken, ribs, corn bread, banana pudding; it was the best food of the tour. When we met with the caterer after dinner to talk about the rest of the shows, and when he heard how much Zukoski was willing to pay them, they dejectedly agreed to do the remaining three shows. But the variety and quality of that first meal in San Antonio degraded with each show, and by the last one it was basically white bread, gravy, and beans.

The next show was at the Mercedes Showgrounds, a rodeo not far from the Mexican border in the Rio Grande Valley. The show had barely sold 3000 tickets, and we got crushed; there was no way we could break even in Texas, and the promoter was going to lose a serious chunk of money. It's never great having a show bomb, but doing it in a fiery Tex-Mex dust pit made it unbearable. I was told that Mexican metal fans loved Slayer, and would come pouring over the border once we opened the doors, but it didn't happen; I stood on a hill looking at the border, and there was nothing and nobody. The only bright spot was the concrete pavilion where we set up the village. It had built-in power, a roof, and was ideal for the tattoo artists. Sean was scheduled to tattoo a local radio DJ live on the air, and once the DJ was laid out upon a table, and Sean started tattooing, Naomi headed across the field to the production office, satisfied that she finally got the village setup right. She was half way there when she heard Sean over the radio.

"Naomi," he said, the radio breaking up.

"Go ahead, Sean," Naomi replied.

"Naom…Flood…Oh my god," and then the radio went dead.

She ran back to find that a flash flood had swamped the pavilion in eighteen inches of water. It hadn't even rained, and no could tell us where the water came from; it just came in like a wave. The best village setup of the tour had lasted ten minutes.

The shows where tattooing worked successfully were the exception, and it was clear we'd need to make changes before next year. The artists were tattooing their customers on the bus, and that could be a solution, though it took away from the village not having the artists there. We had thought about RVs for the artists, but that would have been a considerable expense. We knew tattooing was going to be a challenge, but it was much worse than we imagined. The tattoo artists were fed up, and there was not much I could do about it before the end of the tour.

The local stage crew warned us that because we were so close to the Mexican border, all our buses would be searched by border patrol when we left Mercedes, and that drugs were one of the things they were looking for. We put the word out to all the bands and crew, and whatever wasn't securely hidden was consumed before we left, which produced one of the wilder parties of the tour. Betsy watched from our bus in amazement that so many people could be so fucked up, and the yahooing and cavorting went on right until the busses left. Shannon Larkin, the drummer for Amen, said that Tattoo the Earth was the most debauched tour he had ever been part of, and Mercedes the crowning achievement. I was too burned out to partake. I hid my shit on one of the band equipment trucks, knowing they were probably hiding their shit in one of mine, and fell asleep before we left the venue. I vaguely remember stopping, and flashing blue lights; they searched one out of three buses, and ours wasn't one of them.

We thought we had warned all the bands, but Nashville Pussy hadn't gotten the memo, and were caught by surprise when they saw buses being pulled over. Nashville Pussy's bus had become the party bus for all the bands, and at that moment there were roughly twenty-five individual things that needed to be hidden, including a gravity bong made out of a two-liter Pepsi bottle that then got shoved into a champagne ice cooler. As the bus was being waved over, Ruyter Suys ripped off all her clothes, and answered the knock at the door totally naked, looking like she had just woken up.

"What's up?" she asked them, rubbing her eyes.

"Oh, we're so sorry," one of them said, averting his eyes. "Um, can you, uh, we need to search your…"

"No problem," she said, "Just give me a chance to get dressed."

"Take your time, ma'am. We'll be outside when you're ready."

That gave the band a chance to hide everything, though the search ultimately produced a small amount of weed, and the band was detained at Border Patrol for a few hours. Joining them there were Slayer, whose search also turned up something the border patrol was identifying as heroin, but the band's tour manager was saying was hash, and that it belonged to a crew member. Whatever it was, Ruyter saw Kerry King standing behind glass with arms folded, furious, staring at his tour manager like a super-villain from a cartoon whose laser vision could cut a person in half. Jeff Hanneman and Paul Bostaph were giggling watching spiders fighting in webs on the wall, and Tom Araya and his wife were giggling in their own world. Slayer's bus was impounded, and several crew arrested, and they made it to the next show in Houston just in time to play another rodeo.

The last show in Texas was at an amphitheatre in Dallas. Being in an amphitheatre after three rodeos was like camping for months, and then getting to stay in a five-star hotel. The promoter was rightfully forlorn (we had ruined his summer, to say the least), and as an independent didn't have the kind of cushion to absorb a loss that Clear Channel would. We promised to return next year with a stronger line-up and reduced price to make it up to him; we could not fucking wait to get out of Texas. I spoke to Zukoski on the phone, and he said that with only Red Rocks, Los Angeles, and Phoenix in front of us, we were home free, but it didn't feel that way to me. It was easy for Zukoski to say that from his deck in New Jersey, but I was fucked up from being on the road. The stress, the heat, the losses, the monotony of bus travel were all catching up to me. I hadn't been completely upright and coherent before we'd started, and I definitely didn't improve as we went. A rock doc (a young doctor who writes prescriptions for a fee) showed up in Dallas, and we all had our "examinations." I stocked up on pain pills and sedatives, and the doc's visit helped chill out the entire enterprise. But nothing could chill out Paul Booth. Our relationship had gotten worse, and every washed out village, or dusty rodeo, only created more friction. Filip and Bernie had gone back to Europe after Pontiac, and we had Jack Rudy and Gil Monte traveling with us for the remaining dates. Jack and Gil were old-school, West Coast legends (they were of Henk Schiffmacher's generation), and the vibe among the tattoo artists changed instantly once they were on board. Sean, Filip, and Bernie hadn't bought into Booth's complaining and brooding, and knew we would fix it for the next tour. But Gil and Jack fed into Booth's shit, and Gil and I butted heads.

"Why do you get the back lounge on the tattoo artist's bus," Gil asked me one day in front of the other artists. "Why do you get the privilege?"

"Because I paid for it, Gil," I told him. "You pay for the bus, and you can have the back."

Booth was wound up when we left Texas, and our issues boiled over in Colorado. He just wouldn't stop harping about how the tour was ninety percent music and ten percent tattooing and focusing on trivial problems that were out of my control. I was just trying to get this tour across the finish line, knowing it was just the beginning for us, and that the ultimate goal was for tattooing to take a more prominent role. But I could not get through to him. At a rest stop on the way to Red Rocks, I vented to Sean about Booth and how we had all given him a chance to be part of our thing, that he had done nothing but make it a bummer, and that I'd had it.

"You're the guy, Sean," I told him. "I can't do another tour with Booth. We'll deal with whatever fallout there is, but you're the tattoo artist to lead us."

"Whatever you need me to do, Bro," he said, and we hugged.

As we hugged, I looked over my shoulder, and saw Booth looking at us from the bus. The window was open, and I wasn't sure how much of our conversation he'd heard, but I didn't care. Zukoski had always said that whoever the tattoo artists were on the tour would have no effect on ticket sales, and though I disagreed with him before the tour, I was starting to see his way of thinking. Booth was the most temperamental artist on the tour, tattoo or music, and the reality was I could replace him with any competent unknown artist, and it wouldn't affect the box office. I had given him every opportunity, forgiven all mistakes, and it was never enough.

I was standing backstage at Red Rocks when Booth came over with Gil and Jack to discuss Betsy and I having the back lounge again, and I just snapped.

"You fat fuck," I snapped at Booth. "I'm done with your shit."

Gil said I couldn't talk to Booth like that, and Booth was acting up in arms, and I could see where this was heading, so I walked to the bus to cool off. But they followed me, and soon were joined by the body piercers and Sean. They were surrounding me, and I'm not good surrounded. Gil said I couldn't fire Booth, and I told them they were all fired. Sean wouldn't make eye contact with me, and I fired him too. This was that outsider tattoo bullshit Lyle Tuttle had warned me about. Sean had no choice but to go along with it. It felt like Booth had orchestrated the whole thing just to put Sean in a position where he had to choose between me and the tattoo artists. I went on the bus, and it was just me and Betsy. I told her what was happening, and soon Ronnie was on the bus trying to smooth things over. I told him I'd hire a couple of tattoo artists for the last two shows, and we'll be done with these motherfuckers, and move on. Zukoski got on the phone and said I shouldn't fire the tattoo artists, and that I should skip the show, head to LA, and let him fix what happened. Betsy had been looking forward to Red Rocks and was upset that we had to leave. We, both of us, had gambled and sacrificed to make the tour happen, and now it had turned on us. Tattoo the Earth was a selfless endeavor for me, even though my ego was out of control for some of it. Anything I did was in service to the idea, and now the idea had turned to shit.

I agreed to head to LA, though there was a part of me that wanted to head back to Massachusetts and put all the bullshit behind me.

Ronnie was going to call a cab to take Betsy and me to the airport, but I nixed that, grabbed our bus driver, commandeered the bus, and had him take us to the airport. I never even saw the stage at Red Rocks, and my anger and resentment built as we arrived in LA. The owner of the Agency Group flew in from London along with promoters from Australia, Europe, and Asia to showcase Tattoo the Earth for international tours in 2001, but I was having trouble showing any enthusiasm. Zukoski said the road had swallowed me up, that he'd left me out there too long. He said I'd feel differently once I got home, and that I should play the game for two more shows, and then we could fix it.

I avoided the tattoo artists in San Bernardino (Betsy and I were done traveling on the bus), and Zukoski worked with Booth to get him through the last two shows. I knew why Sean stood there as part of the gang that surrounded me, but I felt betrayed, and we didn't have much to say to each other when we saw each other. Booth had run to Clown and Kerry King, and told them all the hardships the artists had endured, how I didn't give a shit about tattooing, and only cared about money. The last part was ironic since I barely made any money on the tour, and anything we did make was less because of all the money Booth blew on unusable sets he designed. Zukoski had seen plenty of people lose it on the road, and knew it was part of touring, but what Zukoski couldn't abide was Booth going to our employees and airing our dirty laundry. I saw Clown backstage, and he gave me a look that said he didn't want to be dragged into our problems; he had plenty of his own. Booth's antics hurt us with the bands and embarrassed us, and Zukoski and I agreed we had to cut Booth loose for any future tours. Naomi was disappointed by Booth's behavior, and it put her in an uncomfortable position. She said Booth was contrite at Red Rocks. She noted that the village setup, on a giant helicopter pad, had worked well, and that Hare Krishnas brought a ton of vegetarian food for the crew, so she'd had a good day.

The LA show took place in the Orange Grove Center in San Bernardino, and it was an evil show. At one point, someone lit a bonfire in the middle of the moshpit, and the fans danced around it.

"This is your show, huh?" the LA promoter asked me as we looked over the scene.

"At least there's a lot of them," I replied, which was true. We'd sold over 10,000 tickets. "And, you know, none of these kids are going to shoot up their high school tomorrow. They got it out of their system here."

Zukoski was working the Agency Group entourage, who seemed impressed by the attendance and the village, but Zukoski was also speaking to some other agents he'd invited to the show. Zukoski was not happy with Agency Group for a number of reasons but mainly because Kirby had tried to kill the tour before we got it off the ground and overcharged for all his acts. Zukoski was not impressed by the international buyers; he never saw the international opportunities for the concept. I'd always envisioned us playing every corner of the globe, and was pleased the buyers were there, but this was Zukoski's deal. He had gotten us this far, and he had a plan on what could take us to the next level, and he wasn't sure it included Agency Group.

Betsy and I flew to the last date in Phoenix, and the heat in Texas paled in comparison to the furnace blast that hit us in Phoenix. The show took place at the Manzanita Speedway, a legendary dirt racetrack, and ticket sales were light. It was the last date announced, and there'd been some talk about canceling it, but Zukoski made sure it happened. It was unbelievably dry and dusty backstage, and when the sun began to set, with a stack of flattened race cars silhouetted in the background, the whole scene looked like something out of *Mad Max*. It was a particularly violent moshpit, and there was a constant cloud of kicked-up dirt. During Sevendust's set, someone yelled "nigger" at Lajon Witherspoon, and the band stopped. Security moved in on the guy, just as the band jumped off the stage, and the scene almost devolved into a full-on rumble. Lajon had heard this on the tour a few times, and the band had just had it. They were ready to give the racist a good old Atlanta stomping, but the guy was rushed out of the venue.

Just as Slayer started playing, I noticed the sky get dark and ominous, and what looked like a giant red cloud approaching us. The wind was picking up, and the cloud was getting closer. I asked a local standing near me what was happening.

"Oh, that's a haboob," he replied.

"A what?"

"A haboob. It's an Arabic sandstorm."

"You're pulling my leg."

"I'm not," he said and pointed to the stage. "And I would take down those scrims, cover things up, and tie everything down. It's pretty intense when it hits."

When the storm did hit, it produced an almost total blackout. You couldn't see your hand in front of your face, and I had to wrap a T-shirt around my head. Naomi saw the storm coming from the production bus and ran to the village, but there was not much she could do. Slayer played right through it. It looked like Slayer were the house band for the end of the world, and you know, that would have been fine with me. I imagined all the sand turning into a funnel and sucking up the entire speedway, us with it, and the whole fucking thing being washed away until there was nothing left of us but a stray amp and some moldy chicken salad.

Chapter Ten

The Hooey in the Liner Notes

When I got home and opened my bag, a steamy cloud of bugs and dust spewed out, and I chucked most everything inside. All I could think about on the flight back to Massachusetts, as I did the post mortem for the tour, was how we could have made so many wrong moves. I felt only dejection and failure. I could imagine producing more tours, but I could not see going on the road with one again, beyond a couple of nights. Though I'd enjoyed being on the road earlier in my career, being on Tattoo the Earth had sucked. I was kicking myself for having let Booth play me and was generally pissed off at everyone. The sweet moments had been sublime, but few and had occurred in the first few shows. The rest was worry, monotony, and stress. Much of the time I'd been sitting in the tour bus, smoking pot and obsessively watching the Weather Channel. But we'd completed the tour, no one had died, and everyone had gotten paid. I was planning to hold a final meeting with my team, but everyone drifted off after the last show without ceremony. Individually, I told them we wouldn't always be an outsider rogue tour, but that I was glad we were the first year, and honored they were all part of it. By the time we started the next tour, I promised, the fiasco we'd just finished would be a faint memory.

"Don't be so sure about that," our tour manager Ronnie Hausfeld told me when I said that to him. "That was a grueling disaster. Worst tour ever. This shit will haunt me until I die."

Disaster or not, it was in the books. Of the eighteen shows, ticket sales for six had been strong, six okay, six were weak, and all of them were painful in their own way. The first tour was always about possibilities, and I'd never expected to make much money, which was a good thing because there wasn't much money left after all was said and done. We overpaid all the main stage bands (most had their best payday ever), and given extra value to sponsors and vendors; everything we'd done was an investment in the next tour. So many people had told me how rich I was going to be, but I hadn't cared about the money. If money was what I'd cared about I would have stayed at my corporate job. I was trying to build a movement, and an industry, and to change the world. I been part of enough start-ups to know that the first year always sucks, and while I was bent out of shape when I first got home, time gave me more perspective, and I started to come around as we began planning for the next tour.

Zukoski and I met with Steve Martin from Agency Group, and he agreed that we needed to make a change. He asked for a few weeks to develop a plan that didn't include Kirby, and possibly not Slipknot. He said the Agency Group believed in Tattoo the Earth, and talked about how impressed the international promoters had been with the LA show. He wanted to move on from the bad blood. I was still raw from the road and probably bitchier than I needed to be, but you couldn't stay pissed at anyone in the music business very long because everyone was screwing everyone over, and you'd be out of business pretty quick if you were too sensitive.

Zukoski was amenable to hearing their plan but told me that he wasn't sure Agency Group had enough headlining acts to anchor a summer metal festival, and he didn't want to be going to competing agencies for headline talent. He thought there were other agencies that could better represent the tour. But that didn't mean Zukoski wasn't interested in Slipknot. He had become a believer—in the band and in the genre. He thought they were more than a gimmick, and that we could build our future with them. He felt his relationship with Richards was solid, and that Richards saw Tattoo the Earth as a money machine once we worked out the kinks. I wasn't sure about Slipknot. I liked the band and admired them, but I didn't appreciate getting banned in markets, and I wanted to be free of the maelstrom swirling around them. Plus, we had antagonized some big players in music, and I had become more concerned about Richards because I knew Sharon Osbourne would do anything to get Slipknot away from us, but Zukoski said Richards was solid.

In addition to the machinations for the next tour, we had the live album to release in the fall. The recording from Pontiac had turned out to be pretty good, and Richards's brother was putting real money toward distribution and marketing. We decided to use my logo with an overlay of some Art Fusion Experiment drawings for the cover. Fran provided all the photos for the booklet, and I was asked to write something for the liner notes. My first thought was to do a piece on how tattoo artists are cocksuckers and copycats. I couldn't come up with anything to say about the tour that was positive. I had been bursting with creativity the past eighteen months, and now I was dried up. I got drunk, played music, looked at the stars, danced around a fire, but I couldn't write a word. I had nothing left to say, and I was under a deadline and starting to panic. I had some descriptive text I'd written about tattoo warriors and tribes being on a crusade that I came across while scrounging old files for material. I showed it to Betsy, and she said I should submit it.

"It's hooey," I told her. "I don't want to be called out for writing something awful, but I got nothing but hooey."

"It's fine," she said, reading it again. "I've never seen a reviewer ever mention liner notes or anything. No one pays attention to those things."

I submitted it, and the final package and booklet looked fantastic. It was called "Tattoo the Earth: The First Crusade," and though live metal albums typically don't sell very well, there was enthusiasm because Slipknot were moving so many records. The record did okay for what it was, but what hurt it was that Steve Richards had given permission for two Slipknot hits to be included on a compilation album that was released just before ours, and that cost us sales.

The album was widely reviewed, and most weren't bad; one reviewer said the music could pound nails into wood. The album got two and a half stars in *Rolling Stone*, though the reviewer warned readers to "watch out for hooey about warriors and tribes in the liner notes."

While Zukoski prepared for the December agent meetings in LA, I sorted through all the media and reviews we'd gotten for the tour, and it was impressive: decent reviews in the *New York Times*, *Los Angeles Times*, *Boston Globe*, plus hundreds of photos, and a video archive from a videographer I'd hired to travel with us. While my original pitch book had been filled with ideas for a tour in the abstract, now I had a trove of real material—footage, pictures, stats, band blurbs, a live album, press clippings—and it all looked formidable. One thing that had worked on the tour was the bond between the bands and the tattoo artists, and that came across in all the pictures of the musicians with their new tattoos. The record company did a six-minute promo video for the live album, and though the video was bit raunchier than I would have liked, it portrayed Tattoo the Earth as a raucous success.

I called Irving Azoff.

"I see what you've been doing out there, Scott," he said when he picked up the phone.

"I pulled it off, Irving," I said. "I did it."

"What have you actually done?" he replied. "One tour?"

Zukoski and I went to see Slipknot play in New York, and sat down with Richards. He was doing much better compared to when I'd last seen him on the tour, and he told us the band was in for 2001. Now we had to lock the band down. We were going to give them a twenty-five percent cut of all future tours, whether they played the tour or not. If they played on the tour, they would get paid what they normally would get paid for a tour. We shook on it, and our attorney started drawing up the agreement. Richards wanted to do the next tour with Marilyn Manson, and Zukoski got to work to make that happen. Zukoski hated giving away a significant cut of the tour, but I always thought we would end up giving a piece to someone. I just wanted a band that could take us around the world, and the size of my piece wouldn't matter if it got as big as we all thought it would.

Zukoski did the LA agent meetings alone, which was fine with me. I had no travel planned other than a trip to Switzerland to visit Filip and Titine Leu to gauge if they might do the tour without Booth. They hadn't heard about what happened at Red Rocks, and were disappointed that everything had turned to shit. They were cordial when we hung out in Switzerland, and guarded, and said they were open to future tours. Booth was very tight with Filip, and I didn't know if it was possible to extricate Booth from them, but it was worth the try. I thought their commitment and artistry and all-around coolness, represented what Tattoo the Earth was all about.

Zukoski met with all his LA agents for B.B. King, A Walk Down Abbey Road, and now our tour. Zukoski met with agents at William Morris who were interested in representing us, but Zukoski's challenge was switching agencies, and keeping Slipknot as our headliner and partner while they were represented by Agency Group. Zukoski met with Sharon Osbourne on the trip, and she made some overtures about Ozzfest and Tattoo the Earth joining forces, but Zukoski told her we were good, and our tour was just fine on its own. Zukoski made inquiries to Marilyn Manson's people, and we went to go meet his manager at a New York show, and his manager told us they were interested and that we should make them an offer. As much of a struggle as year one had been, year two was falling right into place. We put in substantial offers to Slipknot and Manson, and Zukoski called Manson's manager a few weeks later to follow up about our offer.

"We're in," he said. "As soon as Steve Richards gives me a buzz and confirms that Slipknot is in, we'll sign the contract."

Zukoski could sense we were about to close the deal for 2001 and called Richards right away to tell him to call and confirm for Manson.

"Ah, I may need to hold off on that," Richards said. "Ozzfest doubled both of the offers, and I need to think about it."

And that was that.

Any hopes for the 2001 tour we had planned were dead. There was no way to counteract a pissed-off Sharon Osbourne, with Clear Channel and CAA behind her. We could have doubled the offers, but Ozzfest would just double their offers again. Clear Channel had such deep pockets, there was no rational way to compete. Plus, they would keep us out of the amphitheaters and off their radio stations and billboards. They'd spent a couple of million dollars to prevent our second tour from going out. Though I had been faulting Richards and Zukoski's faith in him, there was no way the most powerful players in music were going to let us tour again. Clear Channel, CAA, and Sharon had the gun pointed at our head, and Richards just gave them the bullet, reaping a huge payday and a co-headlining spot on Ozzfest. I doubt Richards even took our twenty-five percent of the tour offer to the band. I think he planned to play us all along.

I was stunned. The odds against getting the first tour off the ground had been so astronomical that once I surmounted them it didn't occur to me that I would have to do it again; I'd never even considered that there wouldn't be a second tour. The B.B. King Blues Festival was in its tenth year, and Zukoski was known as someone who could get tours out year after year. We even had a few major sponsors already lined up. I felt that I had blown it by not insisting we bail on Slipknot. But it was Zukoski's money—he'd put up millions in artist guarantees to put on the first tour—and his part of the enterprise, and he was the one who'd made the first tour happen; I had to follow his instincts. I thought we should regroup, take out a smaller club and theater tour, and rebuild the brand on a grass-roots level. Zukoski had no interest in that. He'd hit a level with Tattoo the Earth, and he wasn't going backward.

I was in denial for a while, thinking there was some way to salvage a 2001 tour, but I soon accepted that the concept as I'd envisioned it for 2001 was over. And, it turned out, plagiarized. Agency Group, still miffed at us for messing with Slipknot, and trying to move the tour to William Morris, decided to launch Tattoo the Planet in Europe in fall 2001 with Slayer and Pantera headlining, and I was powerless to prevent it. I owned the trademark in the US, but not in Europe, and there was nothing I could do other than go on MTV and rant.

It was like suddenly coming down from a great drug trip, or going limp during great sex, or waking up from an amazing dream. You just sit there and try to figure out what the fuck just happened and how can you get it back. I was physically, emotionally, and spiritually spent. I felt betrayed by my own inspiration. And had it even been inspiration? Maybe it was just mental illness and drugs. The wave of self-doubt was as sudden and stunning as the wave of absolute certainty I'd had in the beginning that Tattoo the Earth would happen. I could replay every decision and rationalize things I did or shouldn't have done; I could blame a hundred other people and capitalism and the weather, but it had been my idea, and I'd fucked it up. I had given it everything, and I'd lost, and I had disappointed all the people who made the tour happen, and trusted me to shepherd it further.

"What do we do now?" I asked Zukoski during one of our many

commiserating phone calls. "You've got tours this summer, but I'm not in the music business. What do you think I should do?"

The law banning tattooing in Massachusetts had recently been repealed, and I thought about doing the first tattoo convention in the state, but I was on the outs with the tattoo world and wouldn't even know where to start.

"What would you do?" I asked him.

There was a long pause.

"I'd call Booth."

And that's what I did. Booth and I buried our respective hatchets, and had the first good conversation we'd had since we met. I'm not sure if he was on a new medication, or on the wrong one during the tour, but there was a big difference. I'd never disliked Booth, and I thought he was a great artist. I just needed him to give me a break, and he was finally doing that. Booth felt remorse for Red Rocks, and hoped it didn't contribute to the tour not going out for a second year.

"Nah, that had nothing to do with it," I told him. "The only thing you ruined was the last tour, for me."

In October 2001, we put on the first tattoo convention in Massachusetts, and the Mass Tattoo Festival was a success, despite taking place less than a month after 9/11. Booth talked about canceling, but I said I wasn't in the fucking thing to cancel, and the show was going to go on. We lost some of our international tattoo artists (including Bernie Luther), and didn't do as many customers as I'd hoped, but still drew 8000 people over three days. The US military bombed Afghanistan on the last day of the show, which caused customers to leave immediately; people tend to want to be home when war breaks out. Booth put on a great show, with one of the greatest collection of artists ever assembled, and I got the entire city of Worcester to support it. We had music at a local venue, and tattooed people got discounts all weekend at movies, museums, and restaurants. Filip and Titine came over from Switzerland, and it seemed we were on to a new direction. Booth was still heavy lifting, but most artists are, and I actually felt satisfied after the show.

The show caught people's attention, and in the summer 2002 we put on two three-day tattoo conventions called Tattoo the Earth— in Chicago at Allstate Arena, and in Oakland at the Coliseum Arena (with Clear Channel, if you can believe it). The shows were almost purely tattooing, with a little music, and the setup was groundbreaking. We put a little stage in each corner of the arena floor, and the arena seats created four mini performance areas where we presented contests and demonstrations. We did an opening event at the Oakland Museum of Art, and the Oakland show was co-hosted by Lyle Tuttle. I considered it a major victory to have gotten him on board. I spent a day at his house in Ukiah, California, drinking cheap vodka and grapefruit juice, and he howled as I recounted my tattoo tour travails.

Aesthetically, the shows were phenomenal. Financially, they tanked. Attendance was okay as far as a tattoo show was concerned, but not for an arena, and that was how the promoter treated it. In Oakland, we got in the middle of a dispute between the Teamsters and Clear Channel, and it cost us dearly. A few weeks after our show the Teamsters blocked the Rolling Stones' trucks from entering the Stadium. We lost money on the shows when I needed them to make some. Plus, Zukoski and Booth were going at it—they'd never trusted or liked each other—and the partnership was becoming fractured. I was tiring of Zukoski's games and maneuvers and of Booth's ongoing biker problems, and I was just about done.

Before the summer shows in 2002, Betsy and I had split up. Her experience on the first tour was mixed. She was glad she went but never wanted to do it again. She thought we were all jerks playing our games, didn't want any part of it, and couldn't wait to get the dust off her shoes. She freaked when I started working with Booth again, and I felt she was holding me back from giving one last effort to keep Tattoo the Earth going. We took a break for a few months. I drove out west, and lived in a motel in Pacifica, the fog capital of Northern California, and did the advance work for the Oakland show. When it became clear that the show was going to tank, and I knew it was over, I fell into despair. I did crystal meth for the first time and went on a ten-day run that culminated with a cross-country drive back to Massachusetts. I wanted to cancel the upcoming second convention in Worcester in the fall, but went ahead with it, though by the time the show arrived I was done and walked away from it all. I gave the Worcester show to Booth, but he was never able to put on another. And that was the end of Tattoo the Earth.

***

The first few years after walking away from Tattoo the Earth were a struggle. The meth jag had taken its toll—my comeuppance for underestimating my addiction. I wallowed in pity for almost a year. Then I put on a suit and tie and worked a corporate job for a few years that was just fucking horrible.

I gradually snapped out of it, found work in academia that I enjoyed for a while, and was part of an academic start-up. I started writing, and in 2020 published my first book, a memoir about my closeted heroin days called *Get Off*. I never considered getting back into the music or tattoo business; in fact, I'd never felt like I was ever in those businesses. My skillset has always focused on people, process, and technology, regardless of the industry, and it's the reason I've had success in disparate fields. People are people; process is process; and technology is technology. It's all the same to me, and as long as I believe in what I'm doing, the only adjustment I need to make is to tone, jargon, and wardrobe.

I still have ideas for new tours. One is called Armageddon on Ice. It would be a fucked-up Ice Capades for metal fans with live music, mutant hockey, and zombie figure skating. But I'm not willing to do what's needed to make it happen, and unless you are willing to throw 100 percent of yourself into a start-up, you have no business doing it.

I've been able to stay off hard drugs, for the most part, and still smoke copious amounts of pot. I look at addiction as a chronic illness that, if managed correctly with a multi-disciplinary approach, flares up every now and then, but doesn't have to kill you. I haven't had a flare up for years, or a drink for over ten, and I got my Hepatitis C cured, so I consider myself fortunate to have survived to still be here, writing this.

Many of those connected to Tattoo the Earth weren't so lucky. Slipknot's manager, Steve Richards, died of his brain tumor in 2004. Slipknot cofounders Paul Grey and Joey Jordison, Jeff Hanneman from Slayer, and Scott Weiland from Stone Temple Pilots all died young and from the lifestyle. Sean Vasquez died of a heart attack in London in 2021. He and I never spoke again after our fallout at Tattoo the Earth, but I remember him with love and gratitude for what we did together.

I'm able to be philosophical now about Tattoo the Earth, but it took a while to get there. I beat myself and "what if I'd…?" myself into many sleepless nights. But I accept now that it just wasn't meant to be, and nothing I could have done would have changed that. I now consider Tattoo the Earth a successful failure. Just getting it off the ground, seeing it through until it was real, proving to myself that I could do it, was in many ways enough for me. It may have been a one-hit wonder, but at least I had a hit, and I've walked the earth differently since having had one.

I've always been successful in my career getting shit off the ground but not as much sustaining it long term, and I've learned to adjust my goals and expectations. And I stopped analyzing whether Tattoo the Earth was mystical inspiration or the result of mental illness or drugs. I now understand that it's all part of me, and I'm okay with that.

So is Betsy. She and I reconciled after the disastrous shows in 2002, had a son in 2007, and are still together today. She got a Ph.D.

in psychology from Harvard, and taught at Columbia University for a while. She's a brilliant person, her time spent with me doing stupid shit notwithstanding.

***

During my meth-fueled cross-country drive back to Massachusetts after the Oakland tattoo show in 2002, I stopped in a motel in Des Moines for the night. I hadn't slept for days. It felt like needles when I peed, and I was surviving on nutritional shakes. I sat on the bed, and turned on the TV, which was tuned to a local news station.

"Good news for music fans today," a news report immediately began. "Two years after a ban on concerts was imposed after the infamous Tattoo the Earth Festival with Slipknot, music is coming back to WaterWorks Park."

What were the odds of that happening?

I couldn't stay in the room. I stood up, turned off the TV, and got back on the road. I ran through it all in my head as I drove, all the gory details—the marriage damaged, the money lost, the dream dashed, the organ removed, the jailers bribed, the friendships busted, and the worst nightmares realized—and I thought the same thing then that I still think today: It was the honor of a lifetime, and I'd do all of it again in a second.

***

Tattoo the Earth Tour Schedule

July 15	Portland, OR	Portland Meadows
July 18	Lawrence, KS	Burcham Park
July 20	East Rutherford, NJ	Giants Stadium
July 21	Scranton, PA	Coors Light Amphitheatre
July 22	Boston, MA	Suffolk Downs
July 24	Cleveland, OH	Nautica Stage
July 26	Bridgeview, IL	World Golf Dome
July 27	Des Moines, IA	Waterworks Park
July 28	Somerset, WI	Float Rite Park
July 29	Milwaukee, WI	Rave Complex
July 30	Pontiac, MI	Phoenix Plaza
Aug 2	San Antonio, TX	Far West
Aug 4	Mercedes, TX	Mercedes Showgrounds
Aug 5	Houston, TX	Pasadena Fairgrounds
Aug 6	Dallas, TX	Starplex Amphitheatre
Aug 10	Morrison, CO	Red Rocks
Aug 12	San Bernardino, CA	Orange Pavilion
Aug 13	Phoenix, AR	Manzanita Speedway

Tattoo the Earth 2000 Tour Vital Stats

Number of shows: 18

Number of miles: 9,736

Gallons of ink: 4.5

Number of times motherfucker was said on stage: 42,639

Number of old ladies complaining about language: 5

Worst crew food experience: corn dog in Nebraska

Number of pizzas ordered for Slayer: 78

Number of people carried away in a Port-o-John: 1

Best name for a Porto-John: Honey Bucket

Main Stage Bands
Metallica*
Stone Temple Pilots**
Slipknot
Slayer
Sevendust
Sepultura
Hed PE
Famous

Tattoo Artists
Bernie Luther
Filip Leu
Gil Monte
Jack Rudy
Paul Booth
Sean Vasquez

Second Stage Bands
Nashville Pussy
Mudvayne
Hatebreed
U.P.O.
Full Devil Jacket
Cold
Downset
Amen
Professional Murder Music
Nothingface
Relative Ash
Systematic
The Workhorse Movement
Esham
One Minute Silence

*Giants Stadium only
**Portland Meadows only

TATTOO THE EARTH

ITINERARY

THU	JUL	13	PORTLAND, O R	TRAVEL DAY
FRI	JUL	14	PORTLAND, O R	PREPROD. DAY / PORTLAND MEADOWS
SAT	JUL	15	PORTLAND, O R	PORTLAND MEADOWS
SUN	JUL	16	LAWRENCE, K S	TRAVEL DAY
MON	JUL	17	LAWRENCE, K S	BURCHUM PARK / EVE. LOAD - IN
TUE	JUL	18	LAWRENCE, K S	BURCHUM PARK
WED	JUL	19	EAST RUTHERFORD, N J	TRAVEL DAY
THU	JUL	20	EAST RUTHERFORD, N J	GIANTS STADIUM
FRI	JUL	21	SCRANTON, P A	COORS AMP. @ MONTAGE MOUNTAIN
SAT	JUL	22	EAST BOSTON, MA	SUFFOLK - DOWNS RACETRACK
SUN	JUL	23	CLEVELAND, O H	DAY OFF
MON	JUL	24	CLEVELAND, O H	NAUTICA STAGE
TUE	JUL	25	BRIDGEVIEW, I L	DAY OFF
WED	JUL	26	BRIDGEVIEW, I L	THE WORLD GOLF DOME
THU	JUL	27	DES MONIES, I A	WATER WORKS PARK
FRI	JUL	28	SOMERSET, W I	FLOAT - RITE PARK
SAT	JUL	29	MIWALKEE, W I	THE RAVE COMPLEX
SUN	JUL	30	PONTIAC, M I	PHOENIX CENTER
MON	JUL	31	SAN ANTONIO, T X	TRAVEL DAY
TUE	AUG	1	SAN ANTONIO, T X	DAY OFF
WED	AUG	2	SAN ANTONIO, T X	FAR WEST
THU	AUG	3	MERCEDES, T X	DAY OFF
FRI	AUG	4	MERCEDES, T X	MERCEDES SHOWGROUNDS
SAT	AUG	5	PASADENA, T X	PASADENA FAIRGROUNDS
SUN	AUG	6	DALLAS, T X	FAIR PARK COLISEUM
MON	AUG	7	BOULDER, C O	TRAVEL DAY
TUE	AUG	8	BOULDER, CO	WILLIAMS FIELD
WED	AUG	9	PHOENIX, A Z	TRAVEL DAY
THU	AUG	10	PHOENIX, A Z	DAY OFF
FRI	AUG	11	PHOENIX, A Z	MANZANITA SPEEDWAY
SAT	AUG	12	SAN BERNARDINO, C A	ORANGE PAVILION NAT'L EVENTS CTR
SUN	AUG	13	T B A	T B A

151

TATTOO THE EARTH
TOURING PARTY
MAIN STAGE

PRODUCTION

Ron Hausfeld	Tour / Prod. Manager
Monty Shipman	Main Stage Manager
Mark Lewis	Side Stage Manager
Brett Stern	Security
Scott Owens	Prod. Manager Asst.
Roy Delaker	Village Coordinator
Gabe Chrislock	Vill. Coordinator Asst
Darron Meeks	Village Road Manager
Pat Heines	Crew Chief
Steve Bellow	Staging Tech
Jeff Page	Staging Tech
Patrick Crowley	Staging Tech
Ron Smith	Staging Tech
Ryan Casey	Staging Tech
Scot Minkley	Crew Chief / Sound
Bruce Danz	Asst Monitor Tech
Ron Hurd	System Tech / MS
Tony Gilliard	System Tech / MS
Paul Reinhart	FOH / Tech / SS
Chris Cole	Asst Mon Tech / SS
Josh Schmitz	System Tech / SS
Jeff Smith	Lighting Tech
Dave Naone	Lighting Tech
Marcus Brown	Show Power Tech
Joe Crawford	Bus Driver
TBA	Bus Driver
TBA	Bus Driver
TBA	Bus Driver
TBA	Truck Driver
TBA	Truck Driver
TBA	Truck Driver
TBA	Truck Driver
TBA	Truck Driver
TBA	Truck Driver
TBA	Truck Driver

VILLAGE

Paul Booth	Tattoo Artist
Sean Vasquez	Tattoo Artist
Filip Leu	Tattoo Artist
Bernie Luther	Tattoo Artist
Gill Montie	Tattoo Artist
Jack Rudy	Tattoo Artist
Abel Sanchez	Body Piercing
Tommy Hill	Body Piercing
Mahina	Henna Art
Atsushi	Henna Art
PreciousSlut	Body Painting

SLIPKNOT

Sid Wilson "fiif"	#0
Joey Jordison	#1
Paul Gray	#2
Chris Fehn	#3
James Root	#4
Craig Jones "133"	#5
Shawn Crahan "The Clown"	#6
Mick Thomson	#7
Corey Taylor	#8
Danny Nozell	Tour Manager
Robert Perdomo	Dir. Of World Publicity
Craig Banham	Tour Security
Shawn Economaki	Stage Manager
Eddie Oertell	FOH / Production
Kevin Moran	Monitors / Engineer
Jedd Taub	Tour Lighting
Zhana Gilavich	Production
Anthony Stevens	Percussion Tech
Tony Gray	Percussion Tech
Kevin Miles	Guitar Tech
Brandon Barker	Drum Tech
Chris Gaster	DJ Tech
Stefan Seskis	Photographer / Video
Frank Pope	Dir. Of Special Effects
Rick Brun	Stunt Coordinator

TATTOO THE EARTH
TOURING PARTY (CONT.)
MAIN STAGE

SLIPKNOT (CONT.)	
T B A	Asst. Special Effects
T B A	Lighting Tech
T B A	Lighting Tech
Aaron Scott	Blue Grape Merch.
Pete	Blue Grape Merch.
Jerry Harris	Band Bus Driver
Dave Mabry	Crew Bus Driver #1
T B A	Crew Bus Driver #2
T B A	Semi Driver #1
T B A	Semi Driver #2

SLAYER	
Tom Araya	Vocals / Bass
Kerry King	Guitars
Jeff Hanneman	Guitars
Paul Bostaph	Drums
Ric French	Tour Manager
Greg Bess	Prod. Manager / F O H
Mark Workman	Lighting Designer
Troy Boyer	Stage L / Guitar Tech
Ian Keith	Stage R / Guitar Tech
Chris Lagerborg	Stage / Drum Tech

SEVENDUST	
Lajon	
Witherspoon	Lead Vocals
Morgan Rose	Drums / Vocals
Vinnie Hornsby	Bass
Clint Lowery	Guitar / Vocals
John Connolly	Guitar / Vocals
Michael Maguire	Tour Manager
Sean "Big Red"	
Johnson	F O H Sound
David "Bull"	
Parrish	Guitar Tech
Chris "Rock"	
Gladfelter	Guitar Tech
Joe Fantuccio	Guitar Tech
Norman Costa	Drum Tech
Jay Jay French	Manager

COAL CHAMBER	
Dez	Vocals
Meegs	Guitar / Vocals
Rayna	Bass Guitar
Mikey	Drums
Todd "T"	
Confessore	Tour / Prod. Manager
Paul "Paulie"	
Leavitt	Stage Mgr / Drum
John "Wedge"	
Branon	F O H Engineer
Kurt Schneck	Guitar Tech
Keroppi	Keroppi
T B A	Bus Driver
T B A	Videographer

SEPULTURA	
Igor Cavalera	Drums
Paulo, Jr.	Bass
Andreas Kisser	Guitars
Derrick Green	Vocals
Eduardo "Eddie" Rocha	Tour Manager
Robert "Radar" Gilbreath	Drum Tech
Silvio Gomes	Guitar Tech
Scott "Goody" Goldwine	Monitors
Giovanino "Nino" Notaro	F O H
T B A	Bass Tech

TATTOO THE EARTH
TOURING PARTY (CONT.)
MAIN STAGE

PUYA		FAMOUS	
Party Of 15. Name list not available		Lauren Boqnette	Vocals
		Patrick Sproule	Guitars
(HED)P.E.		Sean E. Demott	Bass
Party Of 10. Name list not available		Christopher Bratton	Drums
		Rob McDormott	Manager
DOWNSET		Bobby Carlton	Manager
Party Of 12. Name list not available			

SIDE STAGE

NASHVILLE PUSSY	MUDVAYNE
Party Of 10. Name list not available	Party Of 10. Name list not available

HATEBREED		FULL DEVIL JACKET	
Jamie Shanahan	Vocals	Josh Brown	Vocals
Sean Martin	Guitars	J. Montoya	Guitars
Lou Richards	Guitars	Kevin Bebout	Bass
Chris Beattie	Bass	Keith Foster	Drums
Rigg Ross	Drums	Michael Reaves	Guitars
Mike Cavalier	Road / Stage Mgr /	Brian Mandigo	Tour Manager
John Papontineuo	Drum Tech	Keith Douglas	Stage Tech
L. Antunucci	Guitar Tech	Jeff Cameron	Manager
Matt Galle	Merch. / Artist	Jeff Cameron	Manager
Aaron Butkiss	Artist Liaison	Pat Carney	Manager
Eric Johnson	Video Coordinator	Steve Miller	Security / Press
Louis Blanco	Band Security		
Larry Rigsby	Bus Driver		

THE WORKHORSE MOVEMENT		U.P.O.	
Matt Kozuch-Rea	Vocals	Shaun Albro	Vocals / Guitar
Chris Sparks	Vocals	Tommy Holt	Drums
Joseph Mackie	Drums	Chris Weber	Guitars
Patrick Bever	Bass	Ben Shirley	Bass / Vocals
Jeffrey Piper	Guitars	David Gibney	Guitar Tech
Michael Piper	Tour Manager	Brendan Hoffman	F O H / Tour Manager

TATTOO THE EARTH

TOURING PARTY (CONT.)
SIDE STAGE

COLD

Scooter Ward	Vocals
Terry Balsamo	Guitars
Sam McCandless	Drums
Kelly Hayes	Guitars
Jeremy Marshall	Bass
Martin Connors	Tech
T B A	Tech
Rob McDermott	Manager

AMEN

Casey Chimielinski	Vocals
John Fahnestock	Bass
Paul Figueroa	Guitars
Sonny Mayo	Guitars
Shannon Larkin	Drums
Bill Fold	Tour Manager
Shane Hall	Drum Tech
T B A	Guitar Tech

SYSTEMATIC

Tim Narducci	Vocals / Guitar
Adam Ruppel	Guitars
Nick St. Denis	Bass
Philip Bailey	Drums
Todd Shear	Tour Manager
Jeff Harris	Stage / Guitar Tech

ONE MINUTE SILENCE

Party Of 8. Name list not available

NOTHINGFACE

Party Of 7. Name list not available

RELATIVE ASH

Mark Harrington	Vocals
Francisco "Junior" Antunez	Guitar
Carlos Salazar	Guitar
Chuck ford	Bass
John Salazar	Drums
Phil Greenwold	Guitar Tech
Dan Mapp	Tour Manager/ Sound
T B A	Bus Driver

TATTOO THE EARTH

SATURDAY, JULY 15 PORTLAND MEADOWS	PORTLAND, O R PACIFIC TIME

VENUE

PORTLAND MEADOWS

1001 N. SCHMEER ROAD
PORTLAND, O R 97217

CAPACITY

20,000

PRODUCTION CREW HOTEL

COURTYARD BY MARRIOTT

1231 N. ANCHOR WAY
PORTLAND, O R 97217

☎ (503) 735-1818

FAX: (503) 735-0888

CTC: CHARLOTTE COVI

VENUE: 1 MILE

STAGE LOAD-IN

BREAKFAST	7:30AM
STAGES & VIL	IN HOUSE
LIGHTS	IN HOUSE
SOUND	IN HOUSE
LUNCH	1:00PM
DOORS	10:30AM
DINNER	4:00PM

PRODUCTION

SITE PROD MGR	LOWL MC GREGER
SITE PROD TEL	(503) 221-0288
SITE PROD FAX	(503) 227-4418
TATTOO TEL-1	(503) 737-1033
TATTOO TEL-2	(503) 737-1034
TATTOO FAX	(503) 737-1038

BANDS' LOAD-IN SEE STAGE MANAGER FOR TODAY'S TIME SCHEDULE

MAIN STAGE SHOWTIMES

FAMOUS	11:45AM - 12:00PM
DOWNSET	12:20PM - 12:45PM
(HED)P.E.	1:05PM - 1:30PM
PUYA	1:50PM - 2:15PM
SEPULTURA	2:35PM - 3:15PM
COAL CHAMBER	3:35PM - 4:15PM
SEVENDUST	4:35PM - 5:20PM
SLAYER	5:40PM - 6:40PM
SLIPKNOT	7:00PM - 8:00PM
CURFEW	8:00PM

SIDE STAGE SHOWTIMES

RELATIVE ASH	11:30AM - 11:50AM
NOTHINGFACE	12:00PM - 12:20PM
SYSTEMATIC	12:30PM - 12:50PM
AMEN	1:10PM - 1:30PM
COLD	1:50PM - 2:10PM
U P O	2:30PM - 2:50PM
WORKHORSE MVMNT	3:10PM - 3:30PM
FULL DEVIL JACKET	3:50PM - 4:10PM
HATEBREED	4:30PM - 4:50PM
MUDVAYNE	5:10PM - 5:30PM
NASHVILLE PUSSY	5:50PM - 6:30PM
CURFEW	7:00PM

AFTER SHOW TRAVEL

NEXT CITY: LAWRENCE

NEXT VENUE: TRAVEL DAY

MILES TO TRAVEL: 1795

TIME ZONE: CENTRAL TIME

TATTOO THE EARTH

TUESDAY, JULY 18	LAWRENCE, K S
BURCHUM PARK	CENTRAL TIME

VENUE

BURCHUM PARK

2ND STREET & INDIANA STREET
LAWRENCE, K S 66044

CAPACITY

8,000

PRODUCTION CREW HOTEL

HOLIDAY INN

200 MC DONALD DRIVE
LAWRENCE, K S 66044

☎ (785) 841-7077

FAX: (785) 841-2799

CTC: STEPHANIE BOLLER

VENUE: 2 MILES

STAGE LOAD-IN

BREAKFAST	9:00AM
STAGES & VIL	IN HOUSE
LIGHTS	IN HOUSE
SOUND	IN HOUSE
LUNCH	1:00PM
DOORS	12:00PM
DINNER	4:00PM

PRODUCTION

SITE PROD MGR	JOHN BROOKS
SITE PROD TEL	(785) 838-9189
SITE PROD FAX	N/A
TATTOO TEL-1	CEL. TBA
TATTOO TEL-2	CEL. TBA
TATTOO FAX	CEL. TBA

BANDS' LOAD-IN SEE STAGE MANAGER FOR TODAY'S TIME SCHEDULE

MAIN STAGE SHOWTIMES

FAMOUS	12:30PM - 12:45PM
DOWNSET	1:05PM - 1:30PM
(HED)P.E.	1:50PM - 2:15PM
PUYA	2:35PM - 3:00PM
SEPULTURA	3:20PM - 4:00PM
COAL CHAMBER	4:20PM - 5:00PM
SEVENDUST	5:20PM - 6:05PM
SLAYER	6:25PM - 7:25PM
SLIPKNOT	7:45PM - 8:45PM
CURFEW	9:00PM

SIDE STAGE SHOWTIMES

HATEBREED	12:00PM - 12:20PM
RELATIVE ASH	12:30PM - 12:50PM
NOTHINGFACE	1:00PM - 1:20PM
SYSTEMATIC	1:40PM - 2:00PM
AMEN	2:20PM - 2:40PM
COLD	3:00PM - 3:20PM
U P O	3:40PM - 4:00PM
WORKHORSE MVMNT	4:20PM - 4:40PM
FULL DEVIL JACKET	5:00PM - 5:20PM
MUDVAYNE	5:40PM - 6:00PM
NASHVILLE PUSSY	6:20PM - 7:00PM
CURFEW	7:30PM

AFTER SHOW TRAVEL

NEXT CITY: EAST RUTHERFORD

NEXT VENUE: TRAVEL DAY

MILES TO TRAVEL: 1251

TIME ZONE: EASTERN TIME

 LAST NOTICE: ATTENTION ALL ARTIST & CREW: TODAY, JULY 18TH, ALL BUSES AND TRUCKS MUST BE IN BURCHUM PARK BEFORE 11:30 AM TO BE ABLE TO PARK BACKSTAGE. OTHERWISE, YOUR VEHICLES WILL BE DIRECTED TO ALTERNATIVE PARKING AND YOU'LL HAVE TO WALK MUCH FURTHER TO GET TO THE STAGE.

TATTOO THE EARTH

THURSDAY, JULY 20	EAST RUTHERFORD, N J
GIANTS STADIUM	EASTERN TIME

VENUE

GIANTS STADIUM

50 ROUTE 120
EAST RUTHERFORD, N J 07073

CAPACITY
45,000

PRODUCTION CREW HOTEL

AMERISUTES

575 PARK PLAZA DRIVE
SECAUCUS, N J 07094

☎ (201) 422-9480
FAX: (201) 422-9480
CTC: JUDY LYNN
VENUE: 1 MILE

STAGE LOAD-IN

BREAKFAST	6:00AM
STAGES & VIL	6:00AM
LIGHTS	NONE
SOUND	7:00AM
LUNCH	11:00PM
DOORS	1:00PM
DINNER	2:00PM

PRODUCTION

SITE PROD MGR	NEAL RYAN
SITE PROD TEL	(973) 744-0770
SITE PROD FAX	(973) 744-1054
TATTOO TEL-1	TBA
TATTOO TEL-2	TBA
TATTOO FAX	TBA

METALLICA STAGE SHTIMES

SEPULTURA	4:00PM - 4:30PM
COAL CHAMBER	4:50PM - 5:20PM
SEVENDUST	5:40PM - 6:10PM
SLAYER	6:30PM - 7:20PM
SLIPKNOT	7:40PM - 8:40PM
METALLICA	TBA - TBA

BANDS' LOAD-IN

SEE STAGE MANAGER FOR
TODAY'S TIME SCHEDULE

MAIN STAGE SHOWTIMES

FULL DEVIL JACKET	1:00PM - 1:15PM
HATEBREED	1:20PM - 1:35PM
RELATIVE ASH	1:40PM - 1:55PM
NOTHINGFACE	2:05PM - 2:20PM
FAMOUS	2:30PM - 2:45PM
DOWNSET	2:55PM - 3:10PM
(HED)P.E.	3:20PM - 3:35PM
PUYA	3:45PM - 4:00PM
CURFEW	4:00PM

SIDE STAGE SHOWTIMES

SYSTEMATIC	1:10PM - 1:25PM
AMEN	1:35PM - 1:50PM
COLD	2:00PM - 2:15PM
UPO	2:25PM - 2:40PM
WORKHORSE MVMNT	2:50PM - 3:05PM
MUDVAYNE	3:15PM - 3:30PM
NASHVILLE PUSSY	3:45PM - 4:00PM
CURFEW	4:00PM

AFTER SHOW TRAVEL

NEXT CITY: SCRANTON   MILES TO TRAVEL: 130

NEXT VENUE: COORS AMP. @ MONTAGE MOUNTAIN   TIME ZONE: EASTERN TIME

TATTOO THE EARTH

FRIDAY, JULY 21
COORS AMP. @ MONTAGE MOUNTAIN

SCRANTON, P A
EASTERN TIME

VENUE

COORS AMP. @ MONTAGE MOUNTAIN

1000 MONTAGE MOUNTAIN ROAD
SCRANTON, P A 18503

CAPACITY
18,000

PRODUCTION CREW HOTEL

COURTYARD BY MARRIOTT

16 GLENMAURA NAT'L BLVD.
MOOSIC, P A 18507

☎ (570) 969-2100

FAX: (570) 969-2110

CYC: LAURIE ARGONISH

VENUE: 1 MILE

STAGE LOAD-IN

BREAKFAST	5:30AM
STAGES & VIL	6:00AM
LIGHTS	6:00AM
SOUND	6:00AM
LUNCH	11:00AM
DOORS	11:00AM
DINNER	3:00PM

PRODUCTION

SITE PROD MGR	NEAL RYAN
SITE PROD TEL	(973) 744-0770
SITE PROD FAX	(973) 744-1054
TATTOO TEL-1	(570) 963-7962
TATTOO TEL-2	(570) 963-7963
TATTOO FAX	(570) 963-7964

BANDS' LOAD-IN
SEE STAGE MANAGER FOR TODAY'S TIME SCHEDULE

MAIN STAGE SHOWTIMES

FAMOUS	11:45AM - 12:00PM
DOWNSET	12:20PM - 12:45PM
(HED)P.E.	1:05PM - 1:30PM
PUYA	1:50PM - 2:15PM
SEPULTURA	2:35PM - 3:15PM
COAL CHAMBER	3:35PM - 4:15PM
SEVENDUST	4:35PM - 5:20PM
SLAYER	5:40PM - 6:40PM
SLIPKNOT	7:00PM - 8:00PM
CURFEW	8:00PM

SIDE STAGE SHOWTIMES

U P O	11:00AM - 11:20AM
WORKHORSE MVMNT	11:30AM - 11:50AM
FULL DEVIL JACKET	12:00PM - 12:20PM
HATEBREED	12:40PM - 1:00PM
RELATIVE ASH	1:20PM - 1:40PM
NOTHINGFACE	2:00PM - 2:20PM
SYSTEMATIC	2:40PM - 3:00PM
AMEN	3:20PM - 3:40PM
COLD	4:00PM - 4:20PM
MUDVAYNE	4:40PM - 5:00PM
NASHVILLE PUSSY	5:20PM - 6:00PM
CURFEW	6:30PM

AFTER SHOW TRAVEL

NEXT CITY: EAST BOSTON

NEXT VENUE: SUFFOLK - DOWNS RACETRACK

MILES TO TRAVEL: 292

TIME ZONE: EASTERN TIME

TATTOO THE EARTH

SATURDAY, JULY 22	EAST BOSTON, MA
SUFFOLK - DOWNS RACETRACK	EASTERN TIME

VENUE

SUFFOLK - DOWNS RACETRACK

111 WALDEMER AVENUE
EAST BOSTON, MA 02128

CAPACITY
35,000

PRODUCTION CREW HOTEL

HOWARD JOHNSON

407 SQUIRE ROAD
REVERE, M A 02151

☎ (781) 284-7200
FAX: (781) 289-3176
CTC: JOHN PEREZ
VENUE: TBA

STAGE LOAD-IN

BREAKFAST	6:00AM
STAGES & VIL	6:00AM
LIGHTS	6:00AM
SOUND	8:00AM
LUNCH	11:00AM
DOORS	11:00AM
DINNER	3:00PM

PRODUCTION

SITE PROD MGR	MARK SOCO
SITE PROD TEL	(413) 586-3359
SITE PROD FAX	(413) 586-2955
TATTOO TEL-1	(617) 567-0582
TATTOO TEL-2	(617) 567-0718
TATTOO FAX	(617) 567-6604

BANDS' LOAD-IN SEE STAGE MANAGER FOR TODAY'S TIME SCHEDULE

MAIN STAGE SHOWTIMES

FAMOUS	11:45AM - 12:00PM
DOWNSET	12:20PM - 12:45PM
(HED)P.E.	1:05PM - 1:30PM
PUYA	1:50PM - 2:15PM
SEPULTURA	2:35PM - 3:15PM
COAL CHAMBER	3:35PM - 4:15PM
SEVENDUST	4:35PM - 5:20PM
SLAYER	5:40PM - 6:40PM
SLIPKNOT	7:00PM - 8:00PM
CURFEW	8:00PM

SIDE STAGE SHOWTIMES

COLD	11:00AM - 11:20AM
U P O	11:30AM - 11:50AM
WORKHORSE MVMNT	12:00PM - 12:20PM
FULL DEVIL JACKET	12:40PM - 1:00PM
HATEBREED	1:20PM - 1:40PM
RELATIVE ASH	2:00PM - 2:20PM
NOTHINGFACE	2:40PM - 3:00PM
SYSTEMATIC	3:20PM - 3:40PM
AMEN	4:00PM - 4:20PM
MUDVAYNE	4:40PM - 5:00PM
NASHVILLE PUSSY	5:20PM - 6:00PM
CURFEW	6:30PM

AFTER SHOW TRAVEL

NEXT CITY: CLEVELAND
NEXT VENUE: DAY OFF

MILES TO TRAVEL: 684
TIME ZONE: EASTERN TIME

TATTOO THE EARTH

MONDAY, JULY 24	CLEVELAND, O H
NAUTICA STAGE	EASTERN TIME

VENUE

NAUTICA STAGE
2014 SYCAMORE STREET
CLEVELAND, O H 44113

CAPACITY

7,500

PRODUCTION CREW HOTEL

HOLIDAY INN SELECT
1111 LAKESIDE DRIVE
CLEVELAND, O H 44114

☎ (216) 241-5100
FAX: (216) 241-7437
CTC: CARRIE CORRIGAN
VENUE: 1 MILE

STAGE LOAD-IN

BREAKFAST	6:00AM
STAGES & VIL	IN HOUSE
LIGHTS	7:00AM
SOUND	7:00AM
LUNCH	11:00AM
DOORS	1:00PM
DINNER	2:00AM

PRODUCTION

SITE PROD MGR	FRANK IMHOFF
SITE PROD TEL	(216) 574-2525
SITE PROD FAX	(216) 574-9345
TATTOO TEL-1	(216) 781-4814
TATTOO TEL-2	(216) 781-4815
TATTOO FAX	(216) 621-1422

BANDS' LOAD-IN   SEE STAGE MANAGER FOR TODAY'S TIME SCHEDULE

MAIN STAGE SHOWTIMES

FAMOUS	1:30PM - 1:45PM
DOWNSET	2:05PM - 2:30PM
(HED)P.E.	2:50PM - 3:15PM
PUYA	3:35PM - 3:55PM
SEPULTURA	4:15PM - 4:55PM
COAL CHAMBER	5:15PM - 5:55PM
SEVENDUST	6:15PM - 7:00PM
SLAYER	7:20PM - 8:20PM
SLIPKNOT	8:40PM - 9:40PM
CURFEW	10:00PM

SIDE STAGE SHOWTIMES

AMEN	1:00PM-1:20PM
COLD	1:30PM -1:50PM
U P O	2:00PM-2:20PM
WORKHORSE MVMNT	2:40PM-3:00PM
FULL DEVIL JACKET	3:20PM-3:40PM
HATEBREED	4:00PM-4:20PM
RELATIVE ASH	4:40PM-5:00PM
NOTHINGFACE	5:20PM-5:40PM
SYSTEMATIC	6:00PM-6:20PM
MUDVAYNE	6:40PM-7:00PM
NASHVILLE PUSSY	7:20PM-8:00PM
CURFEW	8:00PM

AFTER SHOW TRAVEL

NEXT CITY: BRIDGEVIEW
NEXT VENUE: DAY OFF

MILES TO TRAVEL: 378
TIME ZONE: CENTRAL TIME

TATTOO THE EARTH

WEDNESDAY, JULY 26	BRIDGEVIEW, I L
THE WORLD GOLF DOME	CENTRAL TIME

VENUE

THE WORLD GOLF DOME

8900 7TH AVENUE

BRIDGEVIEW, I L

CAPACITY
10,000

PRODUCTION CREW HOTEL

BAYMONT INN

12801 S. CICERO

ALSIP, I L 60803

☎ (708) 597-3900

FAX: (708) 597-3979

CTC: SUE MOORE

VENUE: 6 MILES

STAGE LOAD-IN

BREAKFAST	5:30AM
STAGES & VIL	6:00AM
LIGHTS	7:00AM
SOUND	7:00AM
LUNCH	11:30PM
DOORS	12:00PM
DINNER	3:00PM

PRODUCTION

SITE PROD MGR	JIM DARDEN
SITE PROD TEL	(312) 923-2032
SITE PROD FAX	(312) 923-2009
TATTOO TEL-1	TBA
TATTOO TEL-2	TBA
TATTOO FAX	TBA

BANDS' LOAD-IN SEE STAGE MANAGER FOR TODAY'S TIME SCHEDULE

MAIN STAGE SHOWTIMES

FAMOUS	12:45PM - 1:00PM
DOWNSET	1:20PM - 1:45PM
(HED)P.E.	2:05PM - 2:30PM
PUYA	2:50PM - 3:10PM
SEPULTURA	3:30PM - 4:10PM
COAL CHAMBER	4:20PM - 5:00PM
SEVENDUST	5:20PM - 6:05PM
SLAYER	6:25PM - 7:25PM
SLIPKNOT	7:45PM - 8:45PM
CURFEW	9:00PM

SIDE STAGE SHOWTIMES

SYSTEMATIC	12:30PM - 12:50PM
AMEN	1:00PM - 1:20PM
COLD	1:30PM - 1:50PM
U P O	2:10PM - 2:30PM
WORKHORSE MVMNT	2:50PM - 3:10PM
FULL DEVIL JACKET	3:30PM - 3:50PM
HATEBREED	4:10PM - 4:30PM
RELATIVE ASH	4:50PM - 5:10PM
NOTHINGFACE	5:30PM - 5:50PM
MUDVAYNE	6:10PM - 6:30PM
NASHVILLE PUSSY	6:50PM - 7:30PM
CURFEW	7:30PM

AFTER SHOW TRAVEL

NEXT CITY: DES MONIES

NEXT VENUE: WATER WORKS PARK

MILES TO TRAVEL: 341

TIME ZONE: CENTRAL TIME

TATTOO THE EARTH

THURSDAY, JULY 27	DES MONIES, I A
WATER WORKS PARK	CENTRAL TIME

VENUE

WATER WORKS PARK

2201 VALLEY DRIVE

DES MONIES, I A

CAPACITY
15,000

PRODUCTION CREW HOTEL

HOTEL FORT DES MOINES

1000 WALNUT

DES MONIES, I A 50309

☎ (515) 243-1161

FAX: (515) 243-4317

CTC: MELINDA WITKEBOOTH

VENUE: 3 MILES

STAGE LOAD-IN

BREAKFAST	6:30AM
STAGES & VIL	6:00AM
LIGHTS	7:00AM
SOUND	7:00AM
LUNCH	12:00PM
DOORS	11:30PM
DINNER	4:00PM

PRODUCTION

SITE PROD MGR	DAVID VANPUFLAN
SITE PROD TEL	(612) 332-6262
SITE PROD FAX	(312) 913-9728
TATTOO TEL-1	CEL #
TATTOO TEL-2	CEL #
TATTOO FAX	CEL #

BANDS' LOAD-IN SEE STAGE MANAGER FOR TODAY'S TIME SCHEDULE

MAIN STAGE SHOWTIMES

FAMOUS	1:15PM - 1:30PM
DOWNSET	1:50PM - 2:15PM
(HED)P.E.	2:35PM - 3:00PM
PUYA	3:20PM - 3:45PM
SEPULTURA	4:05PM - 4:45PM
COAL CHAMBER	5:05PM - 5:45PM
SEVENDUST	6:05PM - 6:50PM
SLAYER	7:10PM - 8:10PM
SLIPKNOT	8:30PM - 9:30PM
CURFEW	9:30PM

SIDE STAGE SHOWTIMES

NOTHINGFACE	12:30PM - 12:50PM
SYSTEMATIC	1:00PM - 1:20PM
AMEN	1:30PM - 1:50PM
COLD	2:10PM - 2:30PM
U P O	2:40PM - 3:00PM
WORKHORSE MVMNT	3:20PM - 3:40PM
FULL DEVIL JACKET	4:00PM - 4:20PM
HATEBREED	4:40PM - 5:00PM
RELATIVE ASH	5:20PM - 5:40PM
MUDVAYNE	6:00PM - 6:20PM
NASHVILLE PUSSY	6:40PM - 7:30PM
CURFEW	7:30PM

AFTER SHOW TRAVEL

NEXT CITY: SOMERSET

NEXT VENUE: FLOAT - RITE PARK

MILES TO TRAVEL: 278

TIME ZONE: CENTRAL TIME

TATTOO THE EARTH

FRIDAY, JULY 28	SOMERSET, W I
FLOAT - RITE PARK	CENTRAL TIME

VENUE

FLOAT - RITE PARK

701 SPRING STREET

SOMERSET, W I 54025

CAPACITY
30,000

PRODUCTION CREW HOTEL

BEST WESTERN

1818 CRESTVIEW

HUDSON, W I 54018

☎ (715) 388-2394

FAX: (715) 388-3187

CTC: CARLA TIMMERMAN

VENUE: 20 MINUTES

STAGE LOAD-IN

BREAKFAST	6:00AM
STAGES & VIL	6:00AM
LIGHTS	7:00AM
SOUND	7:00AM
LUNCH	11:00AM
DOORS	12:00PM
DINNER	3:00PM

PRODUCTION

SITE PROD MGR	SCOTT OLSON
SITE PROD TEL	(651) 428-7502
SITE PROD FAX	(651) 762-3730
TATTOO TEL-1	(715) 247-4653
TATTOO TEL-2	(715) 247-4654
TATTOO FAX	(715) 247-4655

BANDS' LOAD-IN SEE STAGE MANAGER FOR TODAY'S TIME SCHEDULE

MAIN STAGE SHOWTIMES

FAMOUS	12:45PM - 1:00PM
DOWNSET	1:20PM - 1:45PM
(HED)P.E.	2:05PM - 2:30PM
PUYA	2:50PM - 3:15PM
SEPULTURA	3:35PM - 4:15PM
COAL CHAMBER	4:35PM - 5:15PM
SEVENDUST	5:35PM - 6:20PM
SLAYER	6:40PM - 7:40PM
SLIPKNOT	8:00PM - 9:00PM
CURFEW	9:00PM

SIDE STAGE SHOWTIMES

RELATIVE ASH	12:30PM - 12:45PM
NOTHINGFACE	12:55PM - 1:15PM
SYSTEMATIC	1:25PM - 1:45PM
AMEN	2:05PM - 2:25PM
COLD	2:45PM - 3:05PM
U P O	3:25PM - 3:45PM
WORKHORSE MVMNT	4:05PM - 4:25PM
FULL DEVIL JACKET	4:45PM - 5:05PM
HATEBREED	5:25PM - 5:45PM
MUDVAYNE	6:05PM - 6:25PM
NASHVILLE PUSSY	6:45PM - 7:25PM
CURFEW	7:30PM

AFTER SHOW TRAVEL

NEXT CITY: MIWALKEE

NEXT VENUE: THE RAVE COMPLEX

MILES TO TRAVEL: 327

TIME ZONE: CENTRAL TIME

TATTOO THE EARTH

SATURDAY, JULY 29	MIWALKEE, W I
THE RAVE COMPLEX	CENTRAL TIME

VENUE

THE RAVE COMPLEX

2401 W. WISCONSIN AVENUE
MIWALKEE, W I 53233

CAPACITY
7,000

PRODUCTION CREW HOTEL

AMBASSADOR HOTEL

2308 W. WISCONSIN AVE.
MILWAUKEE, W I 53233

☎ (414) 342-8400
FAX: (414) 931-0279
CTC: T B A
VENUE: 1/2 BLOCK

STAGE LOAD-IN

BREAKFAST	7:30AM
STAGES & VIL	IN HOUSE
LIGHTS	7:00AM
SOUND	8:00AM
LUNCH	11:00AM
DOORS	12:00PM
DINNER	3:00PM

PRODUCTION

SITE PROD MGR	GARY LUMLY
SITE PROD TEL	(414) 342 4536
SITE PROD FAX	N/A
TATTOO TEL-1	(414) 342-4489
TATTOO TEL-2	(414) 342-8422
TATTOO FAX	(414) 342-1475

BANDS' LOAD-IN SEE STAGE MANAGER FOR TODAY'S TIME SCHEDULE

MAIN STAGE SHOWTIMES

FAMOUS	12:45PM - 1:00PM
DOWNSET	1:20PM - 1:45PM
(HED)P.E.	2:05PM - 2:30PM
PUYA	2:50PM - 3:15PM
SEPULTURA	3:25PM - 4:05PM
COAL CHAMBER	4:25PM - 5:05PM
SEVENDUST	5:25PM - 6:10PM
SLAYER	6:30PM - 7:30PM
SLIPKNOT	7:50PM - 8:50PM
CURFEW	9:00PM

SIDE STAGE SHOWTIMES

HATEBREED	12:30PM - 12:50PM
RELATIVE ASH	1:00PM - 1:20PM
NOTHINGFACE	1:30PM - 1:50PM
ONE MINUTE	2:10PM - 2:30PM
AMEN	2:50PM - 3:10PM
COLD	3:30PM - 3:50PM
U P O	4:10PM - 4:30PM
WORKHORSE MVMNT	4:50PM - 5:10PM
FULL DEVIL JACKET	5:30PM - 5:50PM
MUDVAYNE	6:10PM - 6:30PM
NASHVILLE PUSSY	6:50PM - 7:30PM
CURFEW	8:00PM

AFTER SHOW TRAVEL

NEXT CITY: PONTIAC

NEXT VENUE: PHOENIX CENTER

MILES TO TRAVEL: 405

TIME ZONE: EASTERN TIME

TATTOO THE EARTH

SUNDAY, JULY 30	PONTIAC, M I
PHOENIX CENTER	EASTERN TIME

VENUE

PHOENIX CENTER

10 WATER STREET
PONTIAC, M I 48342

CAPACITY

10,000

PRODUCTION CREW HOTEL

COURTYARD

3555 CENTERPOINT PKWY
PONTIAC, M I 48341

☎ (248) 858-9595
FAX: (248) 858-8665
CTC: T B A
VENUE: 1 1/2 MILES

STAGE LOAD-IN

BREAKFAST	6:00AM
STAGES & VIL	6:00AM
LIGHTS	7:00AM
SOUND	7:00AM
LUNCH	11:00AM
DOORS	12:00PM
DINNER	3:00PM

PRODUCTION

SITE PROD MGR	MARRIA ZUKR
SITE PROD TEL	(248) 591-9080
SITE PROD FAX	(248) 591-9086
TATTOO TEL-1	(248) 335-8100
TATTOO TEL-2	(248) 335-8171
TATTOO FAX	(248) 335-9898

BANDS' LOAD-IN SEE STAGE MANAGER FOR TODAY'S TIME SCHEDULE

MAIN STAGE SHOWTIMES

FAMOUS	1:45PM - 2:00PM
DOWNSET	2:20PM - 2:45PM
(HED)P.E.	3:05PM - 3:30PM
PUYA	3:50PM - 4:15PM
SEPULTURA	4:35PM - 5:15PM
COAL CHAMBER	5:35PM - 6:15PM
SEVENDUST	6:35PM - 7:20PM
SLAYER	7:40PM - 8:40PM
SLIPKNOT	9:00PM - 10:00PM
CURFEW	10:00PM

SIDE STAGE SHOWTIMES

FULL DEVIL JACKET	12:30PM - 12:50PM
HATEBREED	1:00PM - 1:20PM
RELATIVE ASH	1:30PM - 1:50PM
NOTHINGFACE	2:10PM - 2:30PM
ONE MINUTE	2:50PM - 3:10PM
AMEN	3:30PM - 3:50PM
COLD	4:10PM - 4:30PM
U P O	4:50PM - 5:10PM
WORKHORSE MVMNT	5:30PM - 5:50PM
MUDVAYNE	6:10PM - 6:30PM
NASHVILLE PUSSY	6:50PM - 7:30PM
CURFEW	7:30PM

AFTER SHOW TRAVEL

NEXT CITY: SAN ANTONIO

NEXT VENUE: TRAVEL DAY

MILES TO TRAVEL: 1212

TIME ZONE: CENTRAL TIME

TATTOO THE EARTH

WEDNESDAY, AUGUST 2	SAN ANTONIO, T X
FAR WEST	CENTRAL TIME

VENUE

FAR WEST

3030 NOTHEAST LOOP

SAN ANTONIO, T X

PRODUCTION CREW HOTEL

CLUB HOTEL BY DOUBLETREE

1111 N. E. LOOP 410

SAN ANTONIO, T X 78209

☎ (210) 828-9031

FAX: (210) 828-3088

CTC: MARILYN BEWINNE

VENUE: 2 MILES

CAPACITY

15,000

STAGE LOAD-IN	
BREAKFAST	6:00AM
STAGES & VIL	6:00AM
LIGHTS	7:00AM
SOUND	7:00AM
LUNCH	11:00AM
DOORS	12:00PM
DINNER	3:00PM

PRODUCTION	
SITE PROD MGR	BILLY MORGAN
SITE PROD TEL	(214) 324-3444
SITE PROD FAX	(214) 324-3556
TATTOO TEL-1	TBA
TATTOO TEL-2	TBA
TATTOO FAX	TBA

BANDS' LOAD-IN SEE STAGE MANAGER FOR TODAY'S TIME SCHEDULE

MAIN STAGE SHOWTIMES	
FAMOUS	12:45PM - 1:00PM
DOWNSET	1:20PM - 1:45PM
(HED)P.E.	2:05PM - 2:30PM
PUYA	2:50PM - 3:15PM
SEPULTURA	3:35PM - 4:15PM
COAL CHAMBER	4:35PM - 5:15PM
SEVENDUST	5:35PM - 6:20PM
SLAYER	6:40PM - 7:40PM
SLIPKNOT	8:00PM - 9:00PM
CURFEW	9:00PM

SIDE STAGE SHOWTIMES	
WORKHORSE MVMNT	12:30PM - 12:50PM
FULL DEVIL JACKET	1:00PM - 1:20PM
HATEBREED	1:30PM - 1:50PM
RELATIVE ASH	2:10PM - 2:30PM
NOTHINGFACE	2:50PM - 3:10PM
ONE MINUTE	3:30PM - 3:50PM
AMEN	4:10PM - 4:30PM
COLD	4:50PM - 5:10PM
U P O	5:30PM - 5:50PM
MUDVAYNE	6:10PM - 6:30PM
NASHVILLE PUSSY	6:50PM - 7:30PM
CURFEW	7:30PM

AFTER SHOW TRAVEL

NEXT CITY: MERCEDES

NEXT VENUE: DAY OFF

MILES TO TRAVEL: 272

TIME ZONE: CENTRAL TIME

TATTOO THE EARTH

FRIDAY, AUGUST 4	MERCEDES, T X
MERCEDES SHOWGROUNDS	CENTRAL TIME

VENUE

MERCEDES SHOWGROUNDS

1000 N. TEXAS AVENUE

MERCEDES, T X 78570

CAPACITY

15,000

PRODUCTION CREW HOTEL

LA QUINTA INN

1002 S. EXPRESSWAY

HARLINGTON, T X 78552

☎ (956) 428-6888

FAX: (956) 425-5840

CTC: OMAR GUEVARA

VENUE: 20 MILES

STAGE LOAD-IN

BREAKFAST	6:00AM
STAGES & VIL	6:00AM
LIGHTS	7:00AM
SOUND	7:00AM
LUNCH	11:00AM
DOORS	12:00PM
DINNER	3:00PM

PRODUCTION

SITE PROD MGR	BILLY MORGAN
SITE PROD TEL	(214) 324-3444
SITE PROD FAX	(214) 324-3556
TATTOO TEL-1	TBA
TATTOO TEL-2	TBA
TATTOO FAX	TBA

BANDS' LOAD-IN
SEE STAGE MANAGER FOR TODAY'S TIME SCHEDULE

MAIN STAGE SHOWTIMES

FAMOUS	12:45PM - 1:00PM
DOWNSET	1:20PM - 1:45PM
(HED)P.E.	2:05PM - 2:30PM
PUYA	2:50PM - 3:15PM
SEPULTURA	3:35PM - 4:15PM
COAL CHAMBER	4:35PM - 5:15PM
SEVENDUST	5:35PM - 6:20PM
SLAYER	6:40PM - 7:40PM
SLIPKNOT	8:00PM - 9:00PM
CURFEW	9:00PM

SIDE STAGE SHOWTIMES

U P O	12:30PM - 12:50PM
WORKHORSE MVMNT	1:00PM - 1:20PM
FULL DEVIL JACKET	1:30PM - 1:50PM
HATEBREED	2:10PM - 2:30PM
RELATIVE ASH	2:50PM - 3:10PM
NOTHINGFACE	3:30PM - 3:50PM
ONE MINUTE	4:10PM - 4:30PM
AMEN	4:50PM - 5:10PM
COLD	5:30PM - 5:50PM
MUDVAYNE	6:10PM - 6:30PM
NASHVILLE PUSSY	6:50PM - 7:30PM
CURFEW	7:30PM

AFTER SHOW TRAVEL

NEXT CITY: PASADENA

NEXT VENUE: PASADENA FAIRGROUNDS

MILES TO TRAVEL: 464

TIME ZONE: CENTRAL TIME

TATTOO THE EARTH

SATURDAY, AUGUST 5	PASADENA, T X
PASADENA FAIRGROUNDS	CENTRAL TIME

VENUE

PASADENA FAIRGROUNDS

7902 FAIRMONT PARK WAY
PASADENA, T X 77507

CAPACITY
15,000

PRODUCTION CREW HOTEL

RADISSON ASTRODOME

8686 KIRBY DRIVE
HOUSTON, T X 77054

☎ (713) 748-3221

FAX: (713) 780-9676

CTC: CAROL CALVO

VENUE: 10 MILES

STAGE LOAD-IN

BREAKFAST	7:00AM
STAGES & VIL	7:00AM
LIGHTS	8:00AM
SOUND	8:00AM
LUNCH	12:00PM
DOORS	12:00PM
DINNER	3:00PM

PRODUCTION

SITE PROD MGR	DAVIES BARID
SITE PROD TEL	TBA
SITE PROD FAX	TBA
TATTOO TEL-1	TBA
TATTOO TEL-2	TBA
TATTOO FAX	TBA

BANDS' LOAD-IN SEE STAGE MANAGER FOR TODAY'S TIME SCHEDULE

MAIN STAGE SHOWTIMES

FAMOUS	12:45PM - 1:00PM
DOWNSET	1:20PM - 1:45PM
(HED)P.E.	2:05PM - 2:30PM
PUYA	2:50PM - 3:15PM
SEPULTURA	3:35PM - 4:15PM
COAL CHAMBER	4:35PM - 5:15PM
SEVENDUST	5:35PM - 6:20PM
SLAYER	6:40PM - 7:40PM
SLIPKNOT	8:00PM - 9:00PM
CURFEW	9:00PM

SIDE STAGE SHOWTIMES

COLD	12:30PM - 12:50PM
U P O	1:00PM - 1:20PM
WORKHORSE MVMNT	1:30PM - 1:50PM
FULL DEVIL JACKET	2:10PM - 2:30PM
HATEBREED	2:50PM - 3:10PM
RELATIVE ASH	3:30PM - 3:50PM
NOTHINGFACE	4:10PM - 4:30PM
ONE MINUTE	4:50PM - 5:10PM
AMEN	5:30PM - 5:50PM
MUDVAYNE	6:10PM - 6:30PM
NASHVILLE PUSSY	6:50PM - 7:30PM
CURFEW	7:30PM

AFTER SHOW TRAVEL

NEXT CITY: DALLAS

NEXT VENUE: FAIR PARK COLISEUM

MILES TO TRAVEL: 241

TIME ZONE: CENTRAL TIME

TATTOO THE EARTH

SUNDAY, AUGUST 6	DALLAS, T X
FAIR PARK COLISEUM	CENTRAL TIME

VENUE

FAIR PARK COLISEUM

1438 COLISEUM DRIVE
DALLAS, T X 75215

CAPACITY
15,000

PRODUCTION CREW HOTEL

HOLIDAY INN ARISTOCRAT

1933 MAIN STREET
DALLAS, T X 75201

☎ (214) 741-7700

FAX: (214) 939-3639

CTC: CAROL CALVO

VENUE: 3 MILES

STAGE LOAD-IN
BREAKFAST	6:00AM
STAGES & VIL	6:00AM
LIGHTS	7:00AM
SOUND	7:00AM
LUNCH	11:00AM
DOORS	12:00PM
DINNER	3:00PM

PRODUCTION
SITE PROD MGR	DAVIES BARID
SITE PROD TEL	TBA
SITE PROD FAX	TBA
TATTOO TEL-1	TBA
TATTOO TEL-2	TBA
TATTOO FAX	TBA

BANDS' LOAD-IN SEE STAGE MANAGER FOR TODAY'S TIME SCHEDULE

MAIN STAGE SHOWTIMES
FAMOUS	12:45PM - 1:00PM
DOWNSET	1:20PM - 1:45PM
(HED)P.E.	2:05PM - 2:30PM
PUYA	2:50PM - 3:15PM
SEPULTURA	3:35PM - 4:15PM
COAL CHAMBER	4:35PM - 5:15PM
SEVENDUST	5:35PM - 6:20PM
SLAYER	6:40PM - 7:40PM
SLIPKNOT	8:00PM - 9:00PM
CURFEW	9:00PM

SIDE STAGE SHOWTIMES
AMEN	12:30PM - 12:50PM
COLD	1:00PM - 1:20PM
U P O	1:30PM - 1:50PM
WORKHORSE MVMNT	2:10PM - 2:30PM
FULL DEVIL JACKET	2:50PM - 3:10PM
HATEBREED	3:30PM - 3:50PM
RELATIVE ASH	4:10PM - 4:30PM
NOTHINGFACE	4:50PM - 5:10PM
ONE MINUTE	5:30PM - 5:50PM
MUDVAYNE	6:10PM - 6:30PM
NASHVILLE PUSSY	6:50PM - 7:30PM
CURFEW	7:30PM

AFTER SHOW TRAVEL

NEXT CITY: BOULDER

NEXT VENUE: TRAVEL DAY

MILES TO TRAVEL: 931

TIME ZONE: MOUNTAIN TIME

TATTOO THE EARTH

TUESDAY, AUGUST 8	BOULDER, CO
WILLIAMS FIELD	MOUNTAIN TIME

VENUE

WILLIAMS FIELD

BASE LINE ROAD & I 36
BOULDER, CO 80309

CAPACITY
10,000

PRODUCTION CREW HOTEL

BEST WESTERN BOULDER

770 28TH STREET
BOULDER, C O 80303

☎ (303) 449-3800
FAX: (303) 402-9118
CTC: STEVE WALLACE
VENUE: ACROSS THE STREET

STAGE LOAD-IN

BREAKFAST	5:30AM
STAGES & VIL	6:00AM
LIGHTS	7:00AM
SOUND	7:00AM
LUNCH	10:30AM
DOORS	12:00PM
DINNER	2:30PM

PRODUCTION

SITE PROD MGR	NICK WILLIAMS
SITE PROD TEL	(303) 753-0770
SITE PROD FAX	(303) 697-0895
TATTOO TEL-1	CEL# T B A
TATTOO TEL-2	CEL# T B A
TATTOO FAX	CEL# T B A

BANDS' LOAD-IN   SEE STAGE MANAGER FOR TODAY'S TIME SCHEDULE

MAIN STAGE SHOWTIMES

FAMOUS	12:45PM - 1:00PM
DOWNSET	1:20PM - 1:45PM
(HED)P.E.	2:05PM - 2:30PM
PUYA	2:50PM - 3:15PM
SEPULTURA	3:35PM - 4:15PM
COAL CHAMBER	4:35PM - 5:15PM
SEVENDUST	5:35PM - 6:20PM
SLAYER	6:40PM - 7:40PM
SLIPKNOT	8:00PM - 9:00PM
CURFEW	9:00PM

SIDE STAGE SHOWTIMES

ONE MINUTE	12:30PM - 12:50PM
AMEN	1:00PM - 1:20PM
COLD	1:30PM - 1:50PM
U P O	2:10PM - 2:30PM
WORKHORSE MVMNT	2:50PM - 3:10PM
FULL DEVIL JACKET	3:30PM - 3:50PM
HATEBREED	4:10PM - 4:30PM
RELATIVE ASH	4:50PM - 5:10PM
NOTHINGFACE	5:30PM - 5:50PM
MUDVAYNE	6:10PM - 6:30PM
NASHVILLE PUSSY	6:50PM - 7:30PM
CURFEW	7:30PM

AFTER SHOW TRAVEL

NEXT CITY: PHOENIX

NEXT VENUE: TRAVEL DAY

MILES TO TRAVEL: 947

TIME ZONE: MOUNTAIN TIME

TATTOO THE EARTH

FRIDAY, AUGUST 11	PHOENIX, A Z
MANZANITA SPEEDWAY	MOUNTAIN TIME

VENUE

MANZANITA SPEEDWAY

35TH AVENUE & BROADWAY
PHOENIX, A Z

CAPACITY

15,000

PRODUCTION CREW HOTEL

BEST WESTERN EXEC PARK

1100 N. CENTRAL AVE.
PHOENIX, A Z 85004

☎ (602) 252-2100

FAX: (602) 340-1989

CTC: RICHARD EMMERLING

VENUE: 10 MINUTES

STAGE LOAD-IN

BREAKFAST	4:30AM
STAGES & VIL	5:00AM
LIGHTS	6:00AM
SOUND	6:00AM
LUNCH	10:00AM
DOORS	11:00AM
DINNER	2:00PM

PRODUCTION

SITE PROD MGR	TERRY DERRY
SITE PROD TEL	(602) 264-4473
SITE PROD FAX	(602) 264-6618
TATTOO TEL-1	T BA
TATTOO TEL-2	T BA
TATTOO FAX	T BA

BANDS' LOAD-IN SEE STAGE MANAGER FOR TODAY'S TIME SCHEDULE

MAIN STAGE SHOWTIMES

FAMOUS	11:45AM - 12:00PM
DOWNSET	12:20PM - 12:45PM
(HED)P.E.	1:05PM - 1:30PM
PUYA	1:50PM - 2:15PM
SEPULTURA	2:35PM - 3:15PM
COAL CHAMBER	3:35PM - 4:15PM
SEVENDUST	4:35PM - 5:20PM
SLAYER	5:40PM - 6:40PM
SLIPKNOT	7:00PM - 8:00PM
CURFEW	8:00PM

SIDE STAGE SHOWTIMES

NOTHINGFACE	11:30AM - 11:50AM
ONE MINUTE	12:00PM - 12:20PM
AMEN	12:30PM - 12:50PM
COLD	1:10PM - 1:30PM
U P O	1:50PM - 2:10PM
WORKHORSE MVMNT	2:30PM - 2:50PM
FULL DEVIL JACKET	3:10PM - 3:30PM
HATEBREED	3:50PM - 4:10PM
RELATIVE ASH	4:30PM - 4:50PM
MUDVAYNE	5:10PM - 5:30PM
NASHVILLE PUSSY	5:50PM - 6:30PM
CURFEW	6:30PM

AFTER SHOW TRAVEL

NEXT CITY: SAN BERNARDINO   MILES TO TRAVEL: 321

NEXT VENUE: ORANGE PAVILION NAT'L EVENTS CTR   TIME ZONE: PACIFIC TIME

TATTOO THE EARTH

SATURDAY, AUGUST 12	SAN BERNARDINO, C A
ORANGE PAVILION NAT'L EVENTS	PACIFIC TIME

VENUE

ORANGE PAVILION NAT'L EVENTS CTR

689 SOUTH E STREET
SAN BERNARDINO, C A 92408

CAPACITY
20,000

PRODUCTION CREW HOTEL

RADISSON HOTEL

295 NORTH E STREET
SAN BERNARDINO, C A

☎ (909) 381-6181
FAX: (909) 381-5288
CTC: TBA
VENUE: 1 MILE

STAGE LOAD-IN

BREAKFAST	5:00AM
STAGES & VIL	5:00AM
LIGHTS	6:00AM
SOUND	6:00AM
LUNCH	11:00AM
DOORS	11:00AM
DINNER	3:00PM

PRODUCTION

SITE PROD MGR	ARON LEVIN
SITE PROD TEL	(323) 769-4679
SITE PROD FAX	(323) 769-4789
TATTOO TEL-1	TBA
TATTOO TEL-2	TBA
TATTOO FAX	TBA

BANDS' LOAD-IN SEE STAGE MANAGER FOR TODAY'S TIME SCHEDULE

MAIN STAGE SHOWTIMES

FAMOUS	11:45AM - 12:00PM
DOWNSET	12:20PM - 12:45PM
(HED)P.E.	1:05PM - 1:30PM
PUYA	1:50PM - 2:15PM
SEPULTURA	2:35PM - 3:15PM
COAL CHAMBER	3:35PM - 4:15PM
SEVENDUST	4:35PM - 5:20PM
SLAYER	5:40PM - 6:40PM
SLIPKNOT	7:00PM - 8:00PM
CURFEW	8:00PM

SIDE STAGE SHOWTIMES

RELATIVE ASH	11:30AM - 11:50PM
NOTHINGFACE	12:00PM - 12:20PM
ONE MINUTE	12:30PM - 12:50PM
AMEN	1:10PM - 1:30PM
COLD	1:50PM - 2:10PM
U P O	2:30PM - 2:50PM
WORKHORSE MVMNT	3:10PM - 3:30PM
FULL DEVIL JACKET	3:50PM - 4:10PM
HATEBREED	4:30PM - 4:50PM
MUDVAYNE	5:10PM - 5:30PM
NASHVILLE PUSSY	5:50PM - 6:30PM
CURFEW	6:30PM

AFTER SHOW TRAVEL

NEXT CITY: SAN FRANSICO
NEXT VENUE: TBA

MILES TO TRAVEL: 438
TIME ZONE: PACIFIC TIME

About the Author

In 2020, Scott Alderman published his first book, a memoir titled *Get Off*. Scott was born in New York City, and has a BA in literature and writing from Columbia University. He lives in Massachusetts with his wife and kid.

Made in the USA
Monee, IL
13 March 2022